FOR ORGANS, PIANOS & ELECTRONIC KEYBOARDS

E-Z PLAY TODAY

225

the **LAWRENCE WELK** Songbook

T0058977

This publication is not for sale in
the EC and/or Australia
or New Zealand.

HAL•LEONARD®
CORPORATION
7777 W. BLUEMOUND RD. P.O. BOX 13819 MILWAUKEE, WI 53213

the LAWRENCE WELK Songbook

Contents

All The Things You Are

(From "VERY WARM FOR MAY")

Registration 2
Rhythm: Ballad or Swing

Words by Oscar Hammerstein II
Music by Jerome Kern

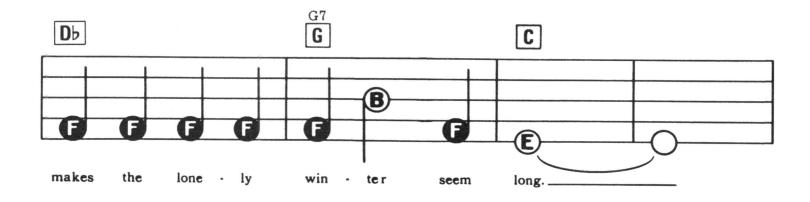

You are the prom-ised kiss of spring-time That

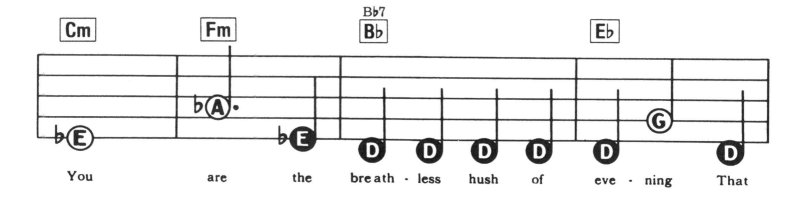

makes the lone-ly win-ter seem long.

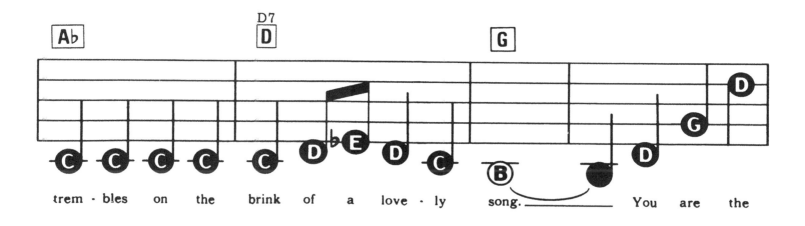

You are the breath-less hush of eve-ning That

trem-bles on the brink of a love-ly song. You are the

5

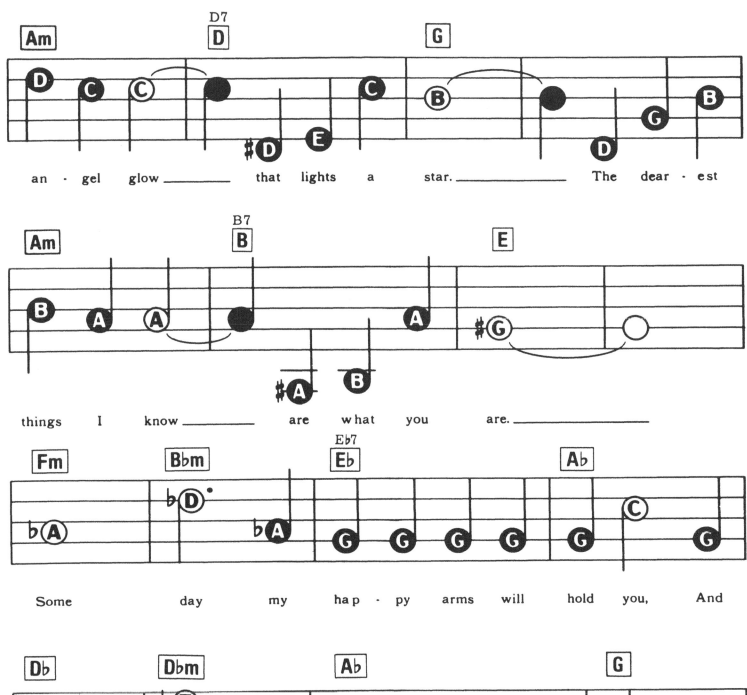

an · gel glow _____ that lights a star. _____ The dear · est

things I know _____ are what you are. _____

Some day my hap · py arms will hold you, And

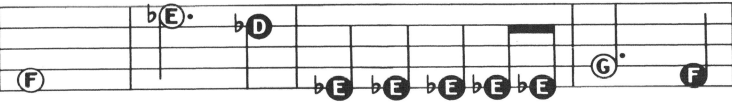

some day I'll know that mo · ment di · vine, When

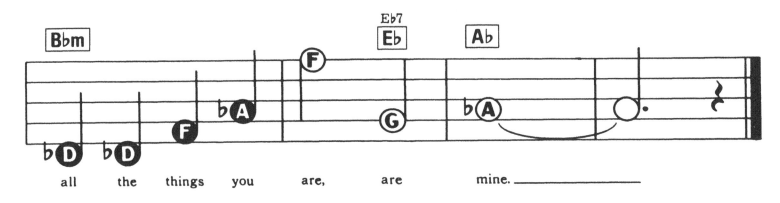

all the things you are, are mine. _____

Apples And Bananas

Registration 4
Rhythm: Latin or Bossa Nova

By Frank Scott

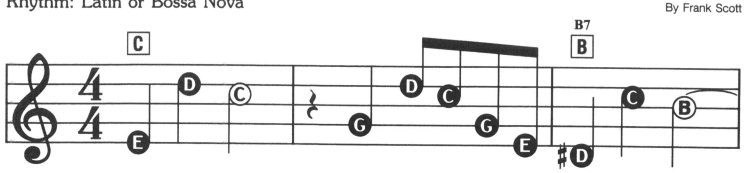

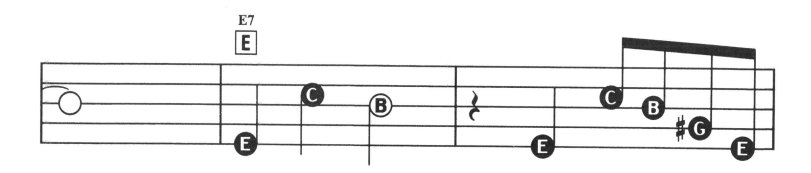

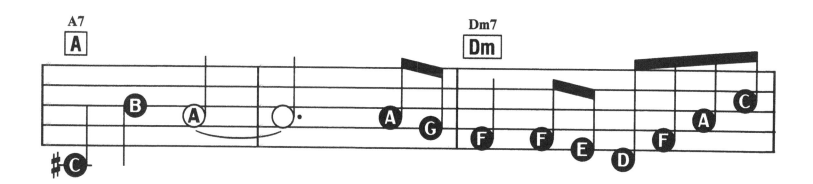

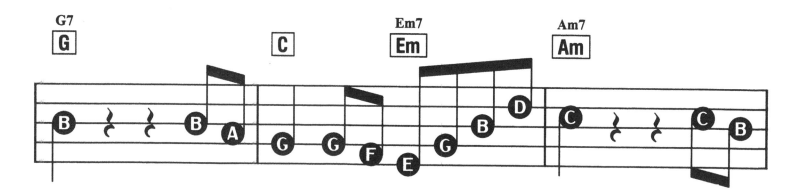

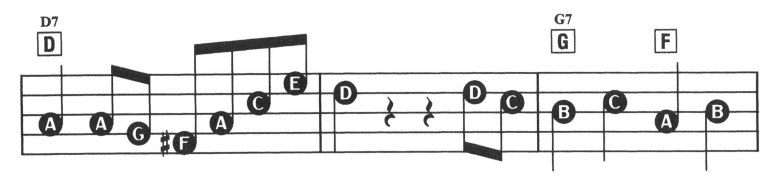

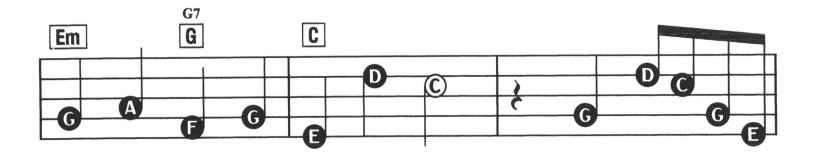

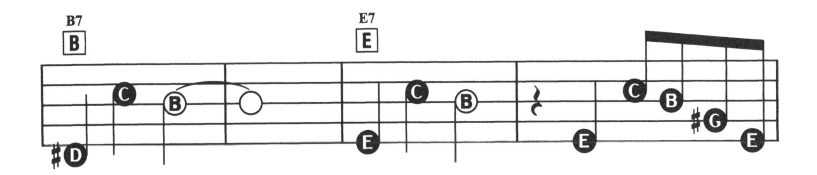

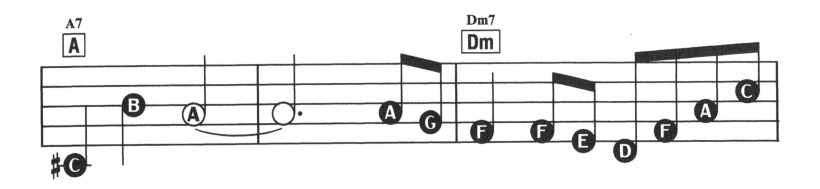

8

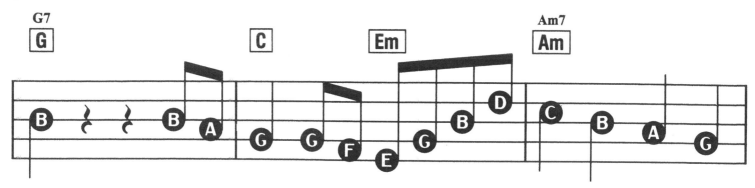

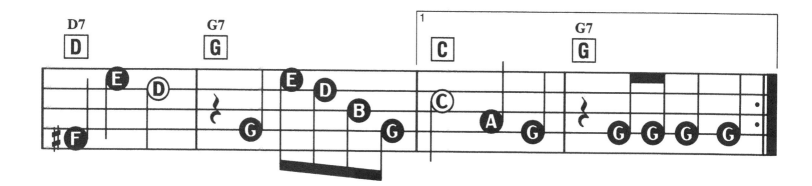

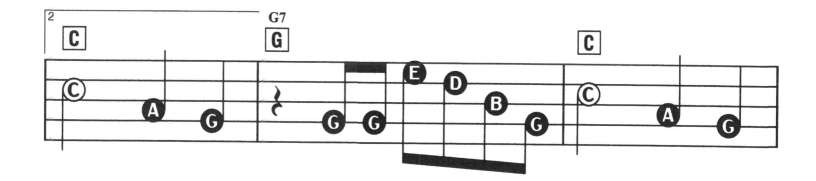

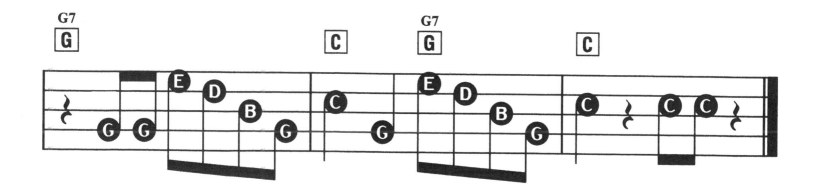

Beyond The Sea
("La Mer")

Registration 7
Rhythm: Slow Rock or Ballad

English Lyric by Jack Lawrence
Music and French Lyric by Charles Trenet

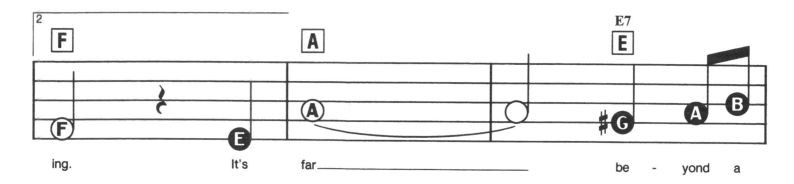

ing.   It's   far   be - yond a

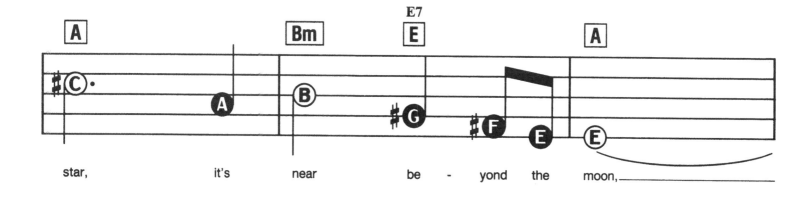

star,   it's   near   be - yond the   moon,

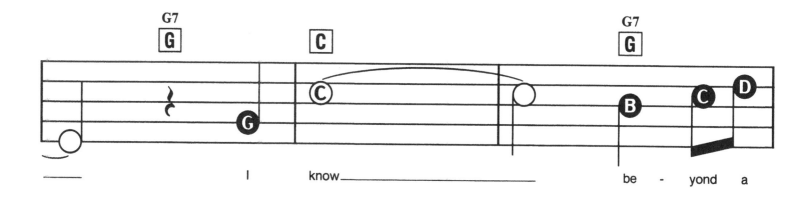

I   know   be - yond a

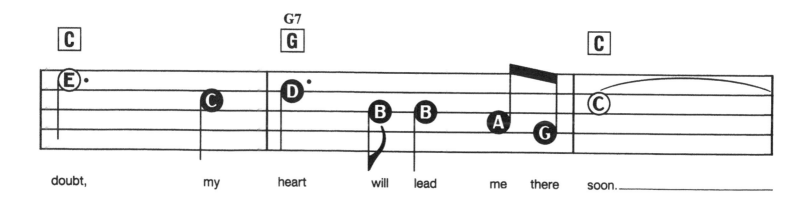

doubt,   my   heart   will   lead   me   there   soon.

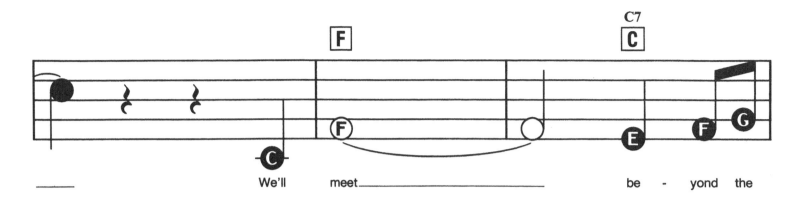

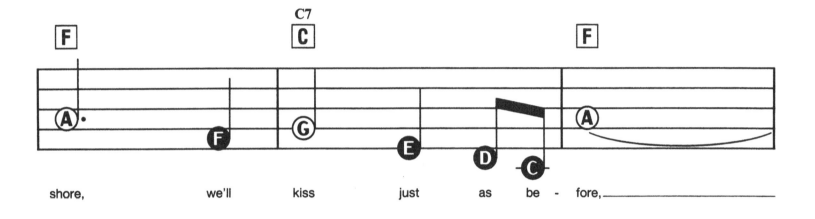

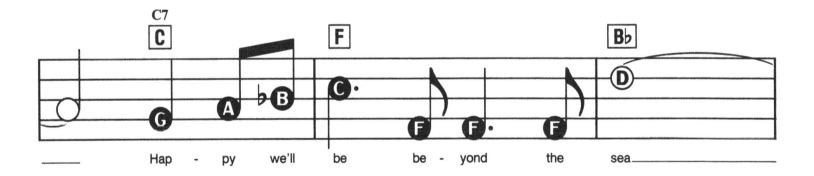

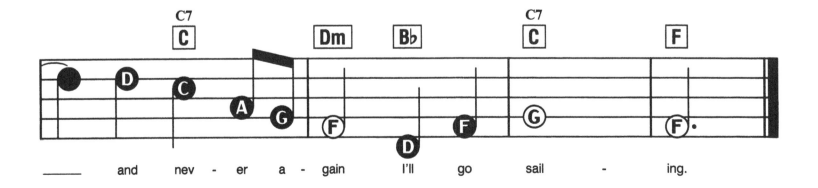

Blue Velvet

Registration 1
Rhythm: Fox Trot or Swing

Words and Music by
Bernie Wayne and Lee Morris

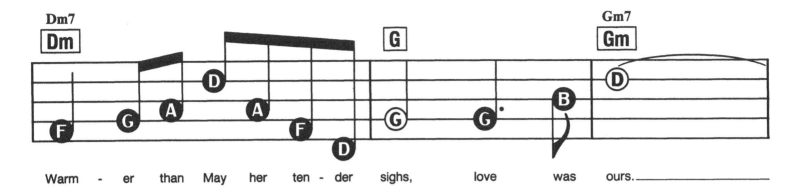

Warm - er than May her ten - der sighs, love was ours._____

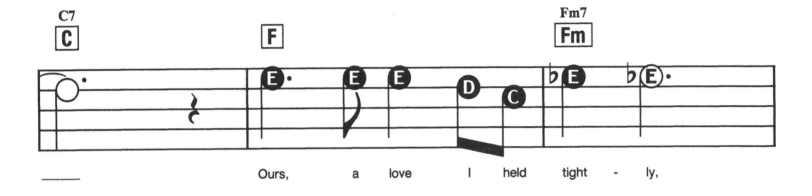

____ Ours, a love I held tight - ly,

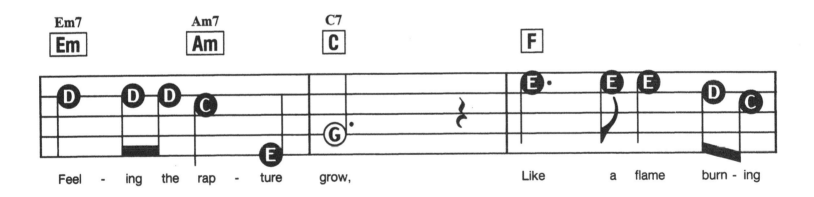

Feel - ing the rap - ture grow, Like a flame burn - ing

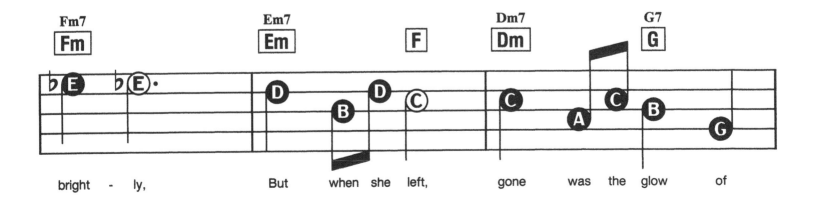

bright - ly, But when she left, gone was the glow of

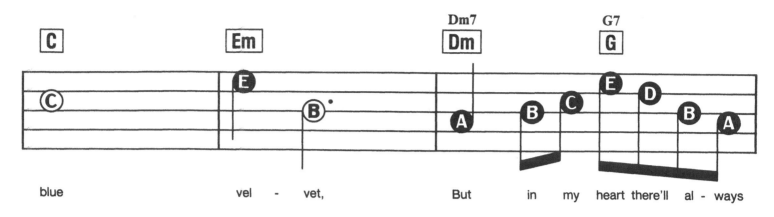

blue   vel - vet,   But   in   my   heart   there'll al - ways

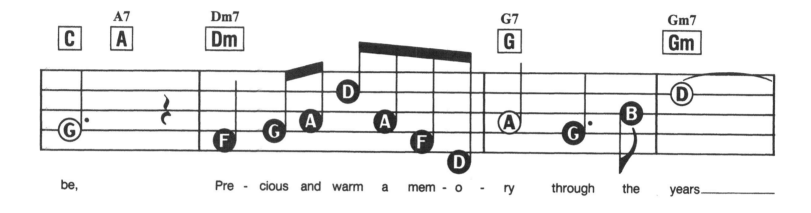

be,   Pre - cious and warm a mem - o - ry through the years_____

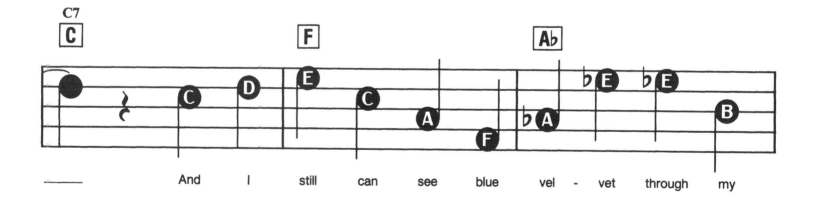

_____ And   I   still   can   see   blue   vel - vet through my

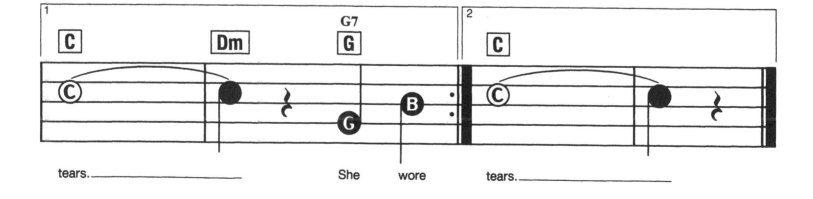

tears._____   She wore tears._____

Bubbles In The Wine

Registration 4
Rhythm: Swing or Jazz

By Bob Calame, Frank Loesser
and Lawrence Welk

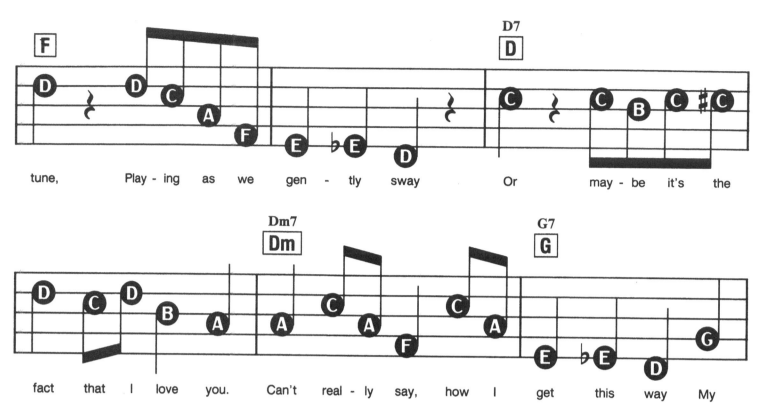

tune, Play - ing as we gen - tly sway Or may - be it's the

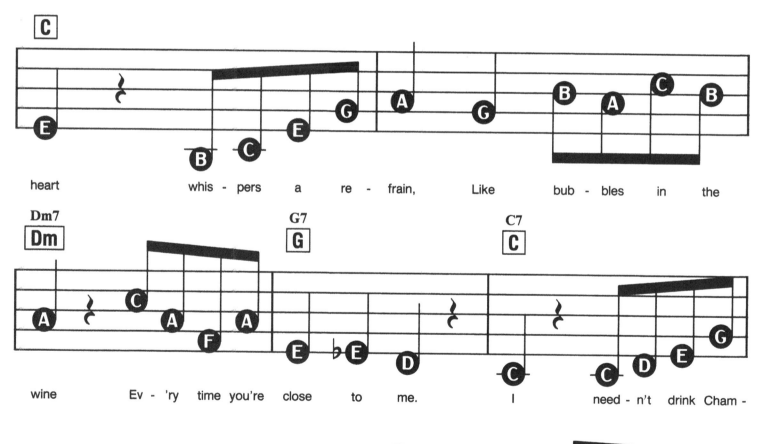

fact that I love you. Can't real - ly say, how I get this way My

heart whis - pers a re - frain, Like bub - bles in the

wine Ev - 'ry time you're close to me. I need - n't drink Cham -

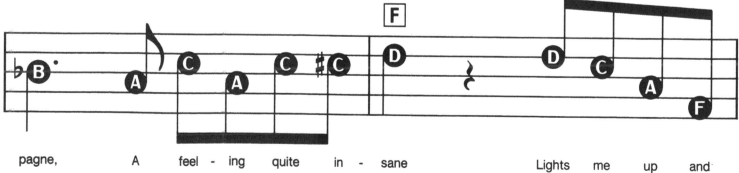

pagne, A feel - ing quite in - sane Lights me up and

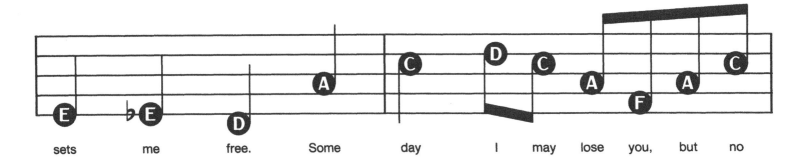

sets   me   free.   Some   day   I   may   lose   you,   but   no

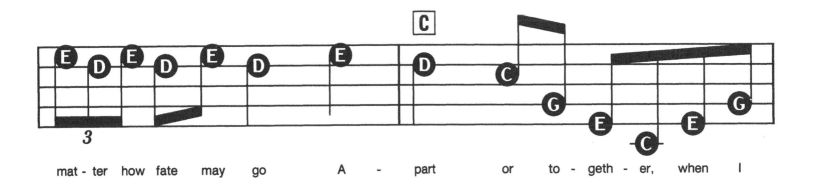

mat - ter   how   fate   may   go   A - part   or   to - geth - er,   when   I

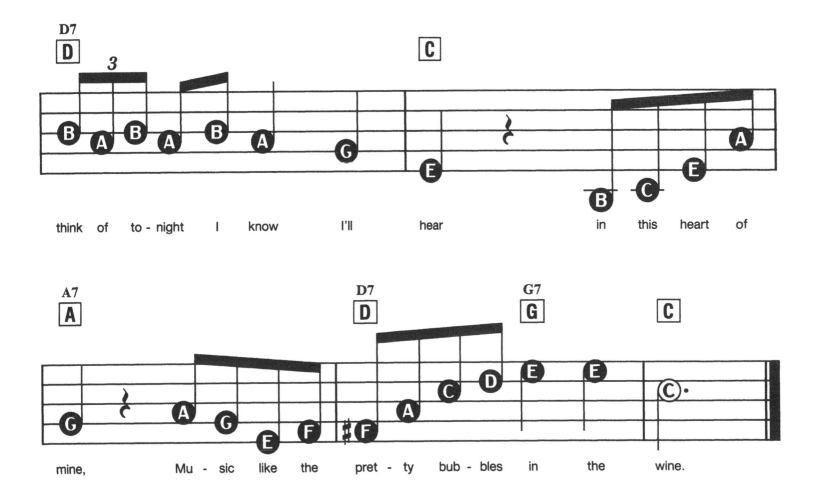

think   of   to - night   I   know   I'll   hear   in   this   heart   of

mine,   Mu - sic   like   the   pret - ty   bub - bles   in   the   wine.

Calcutta
(From the German Hit "KALKUTTA LIEGT AM GANGES")

Registration 4
Rhythm: Samba or Cha-Cha

By Heino Gaze

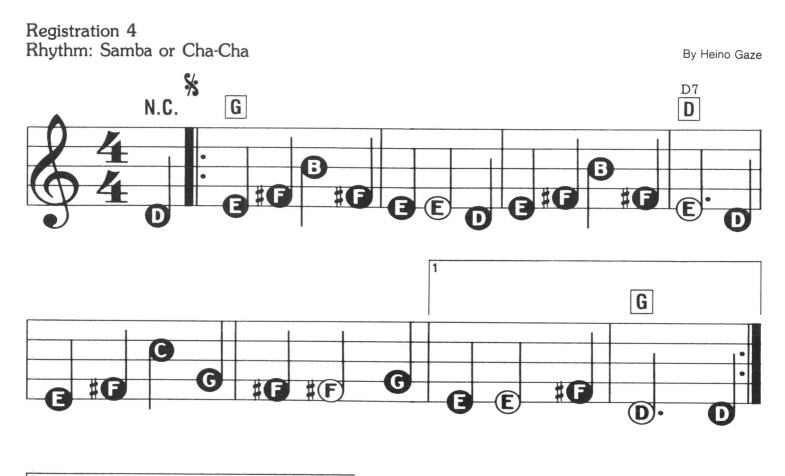

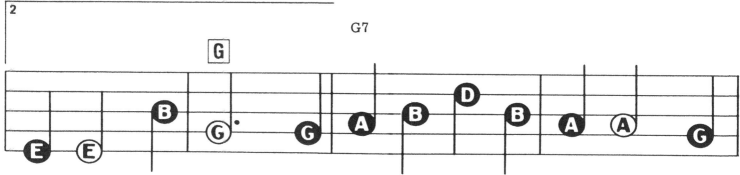

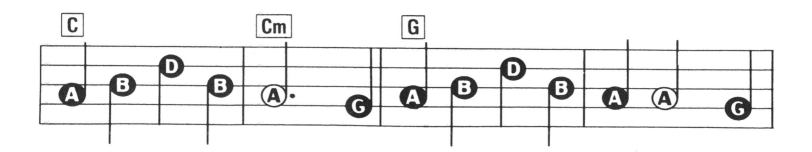

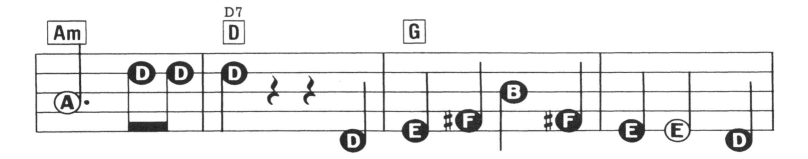

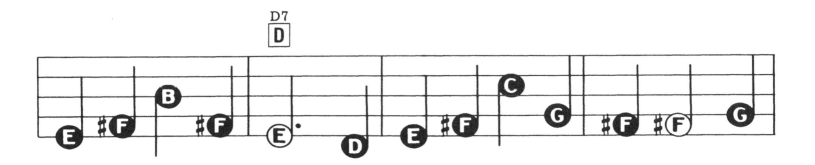

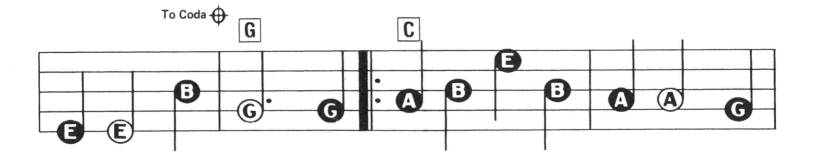

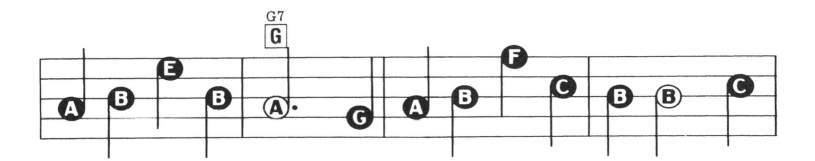

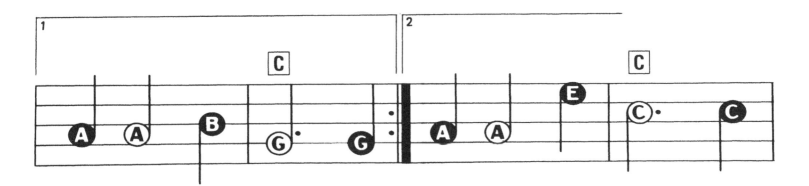

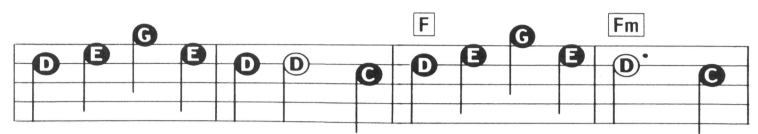

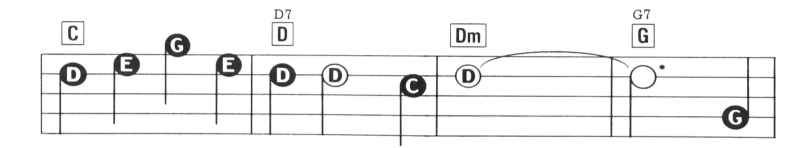

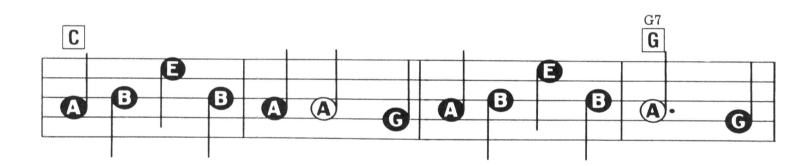

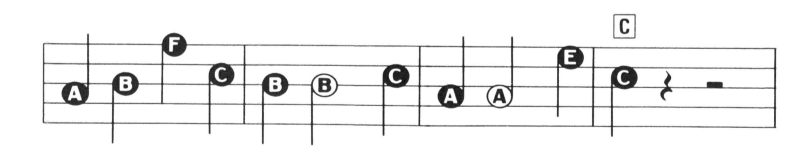

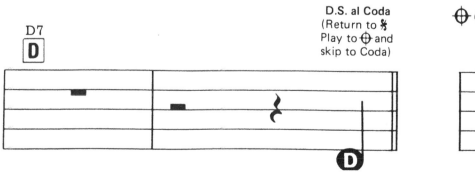

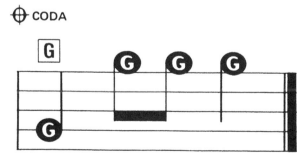

Cherry Pink And
Apple Blossom White

French Words by Jacques Larue
English Words by Mack David
Music by Louiguy

Registration 9
Rhythm: Latin or Rhumba

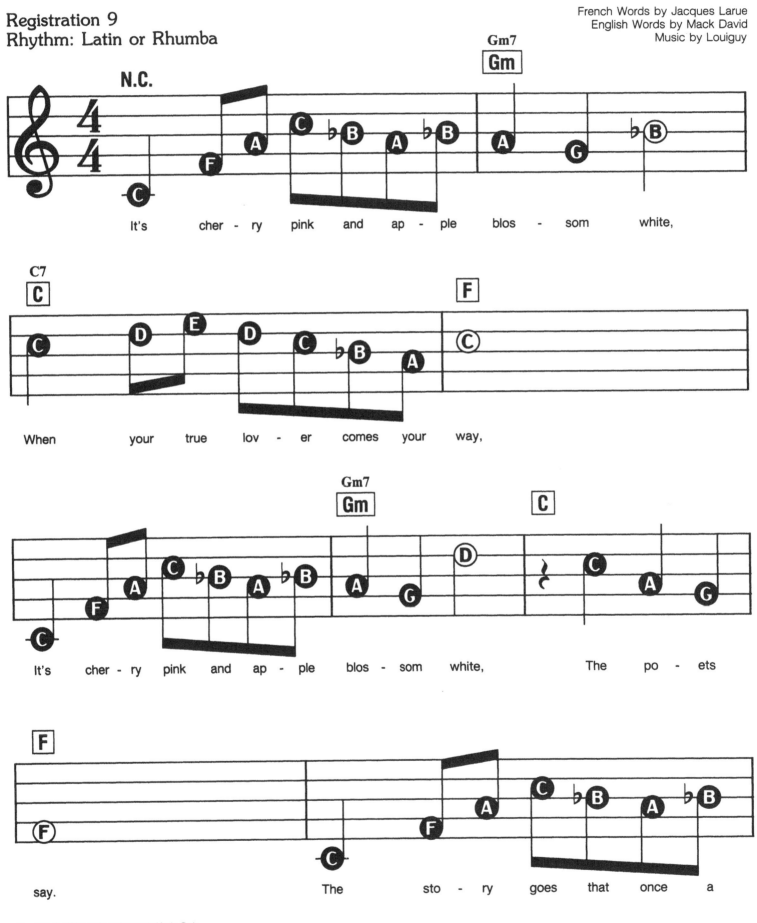

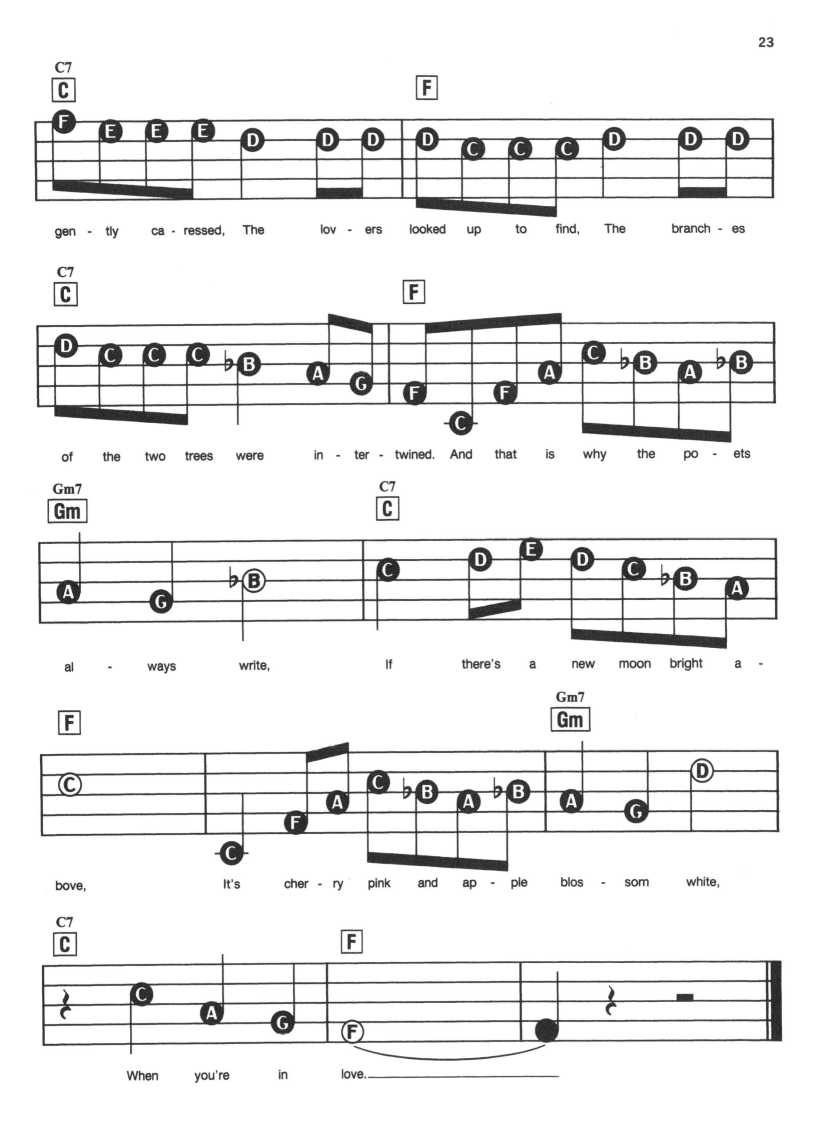

Candy

Registration 4
Rhythm: Fox Trot or Swing

Words and Music by Mack David,
Joan Whitney and Alex Kramer

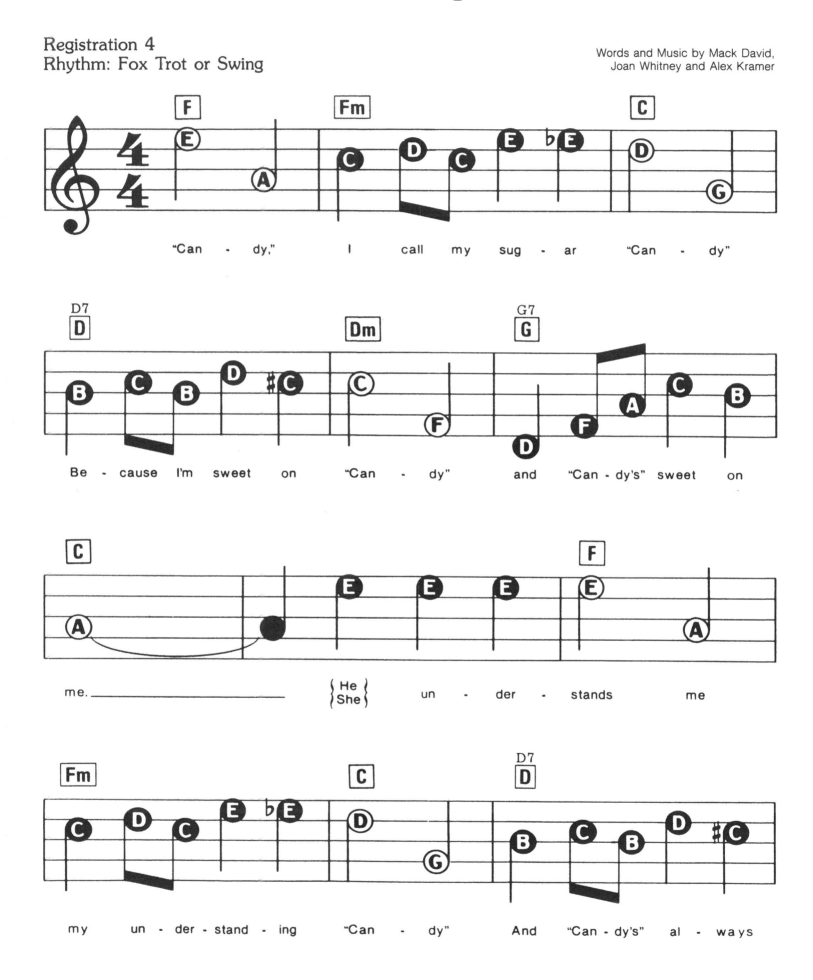

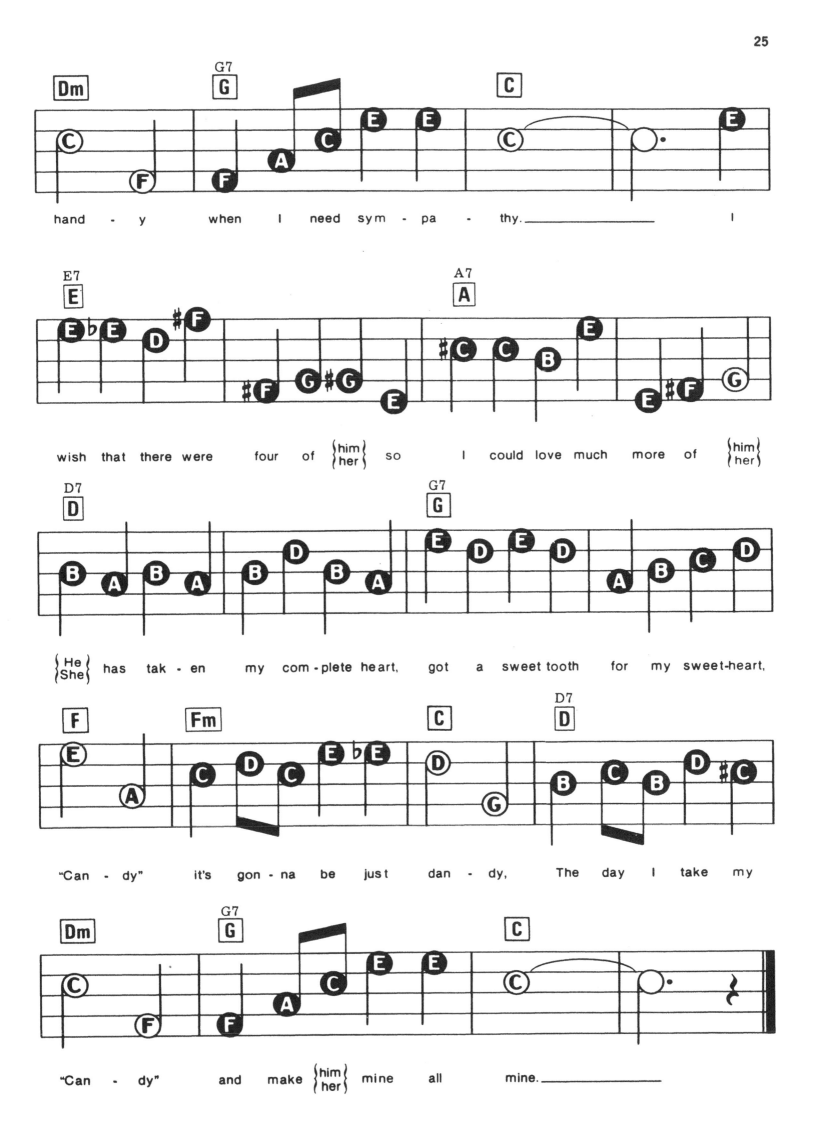

Can't Help Lovin' Dat Man

Registration 5
Rhythm: Ballad or Swing

Words by Oscar Hammerstein II
Music by Jerome Kern

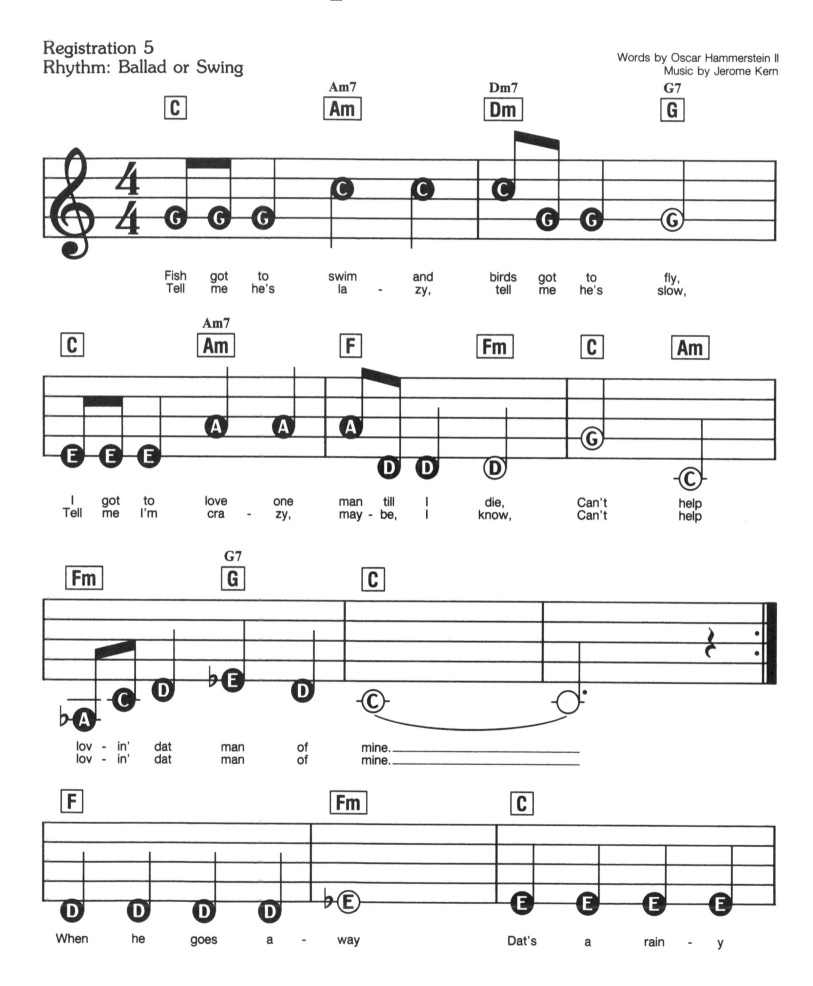

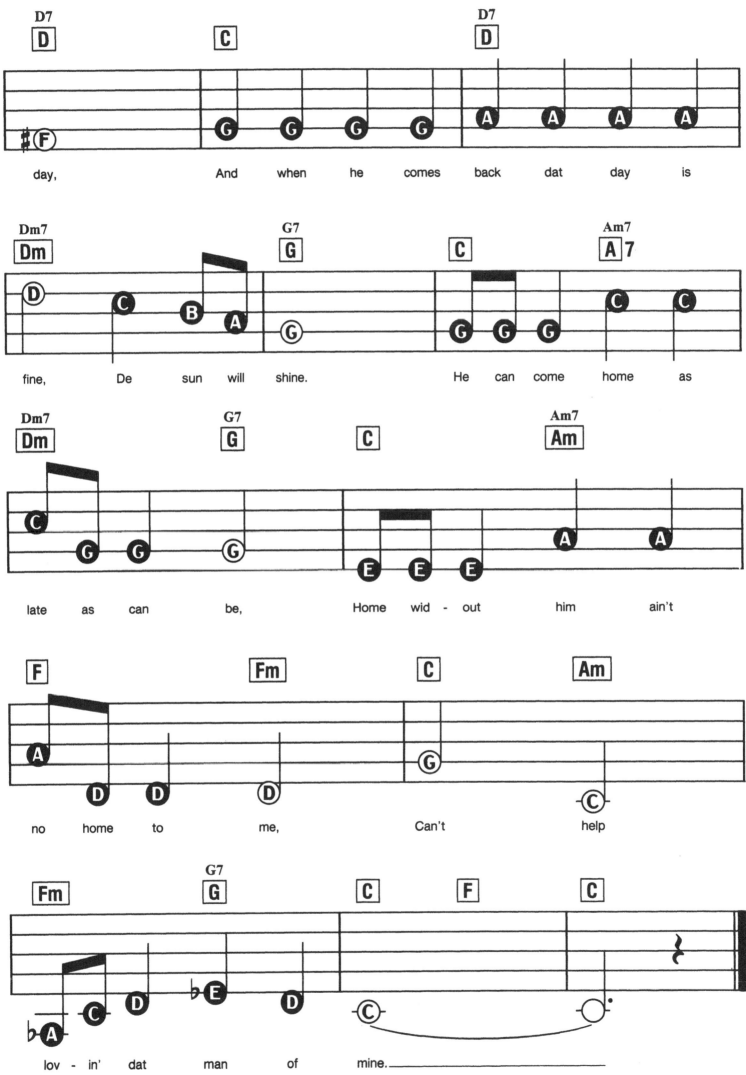

Carioca

Registration 8
Rhythm: Latin or Rhumba

Words by Gus Kahn and Edward Eliscu
Music by Vincent Youmans

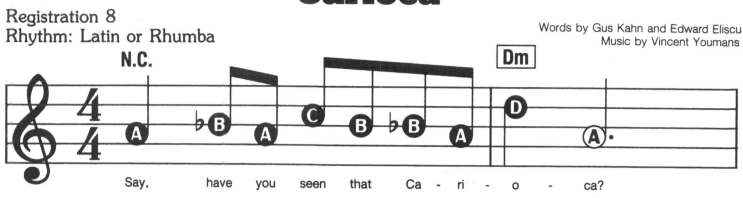

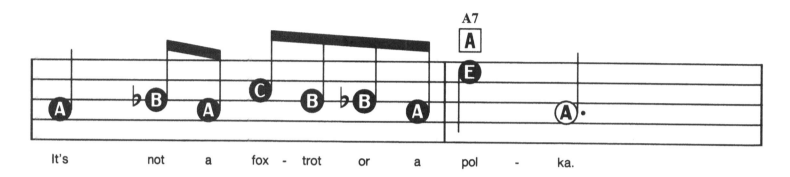

Say, have you seen that Ca - ri - o - ca?

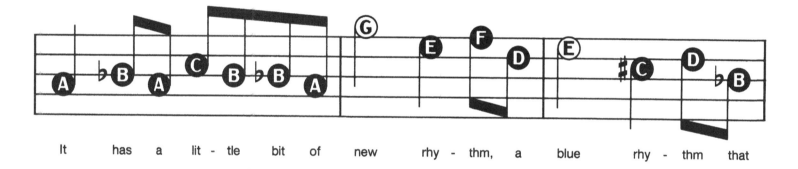

It's not a fox - trot or a pol - ka.

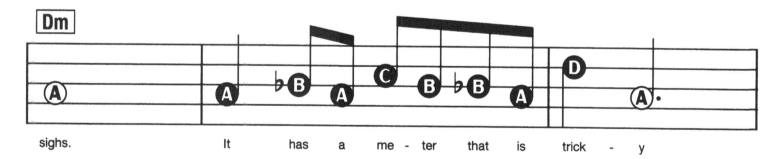

It has a lit - tle bit of new rhy - thm, a blue rhy - thm that

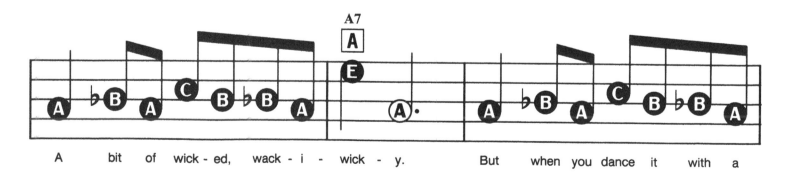

sighs. It has a me - ter that is trick - y

A bit of wick - ed, wack - i - wick - y. But when you dance it with a

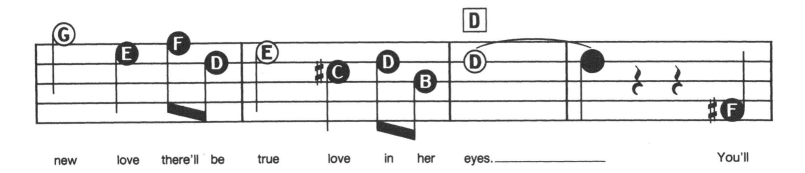

new love there'll be true love in her eyes._____ You'll

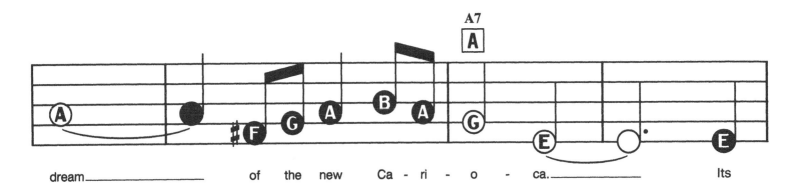

dream_____ of the new Ca - ri - o - ca._____ Its

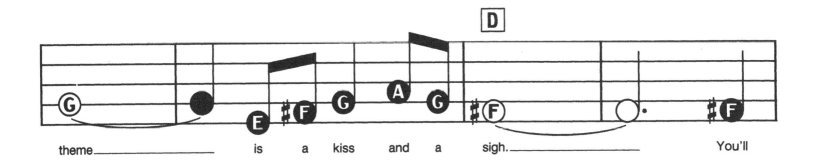

theme_____ is a kiss and a sigh._____ You'll

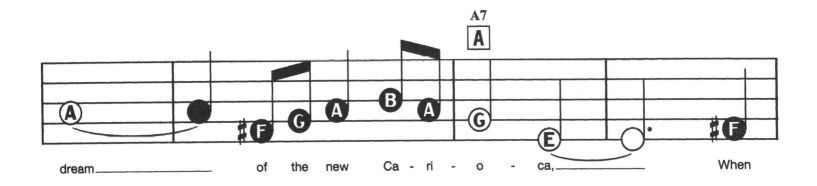

dream_____ of the new Ca - ri - o - ca,_____ When

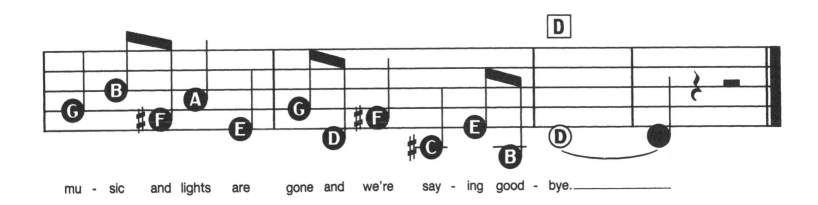

mu - sic and lights are gone and we're say - ing good - bye._____

Champagne Time

Registration 5
Rhythm: Swing or Jazz

Words and Music by
George Cates

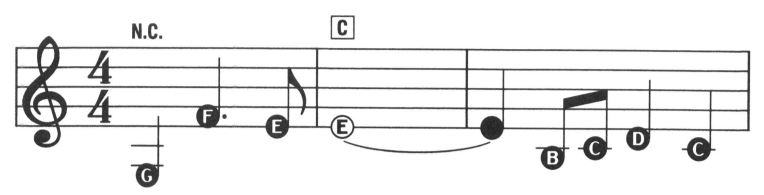

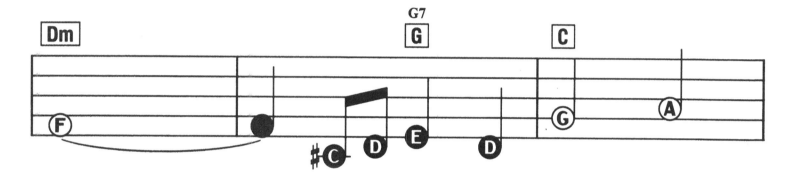

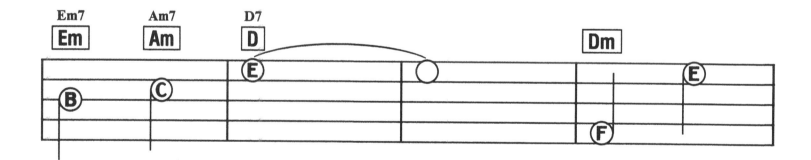

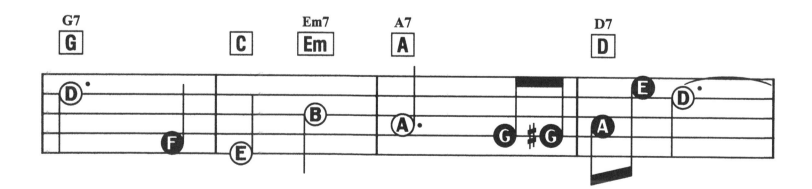

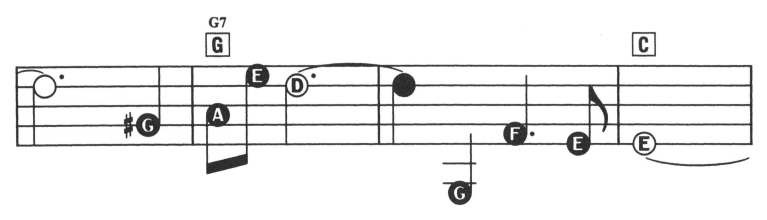

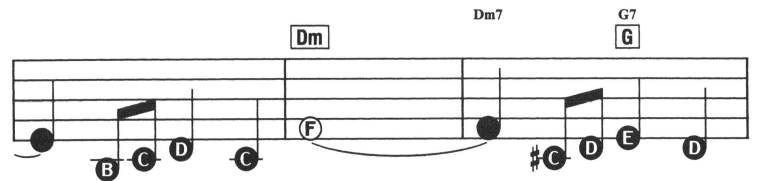

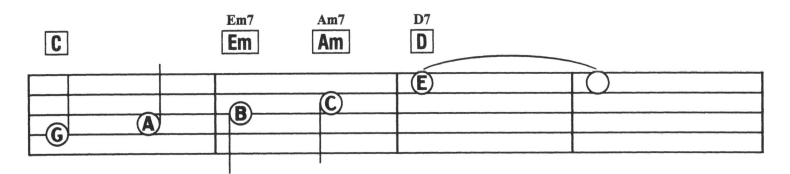

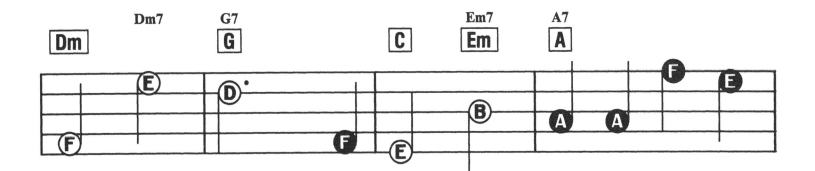

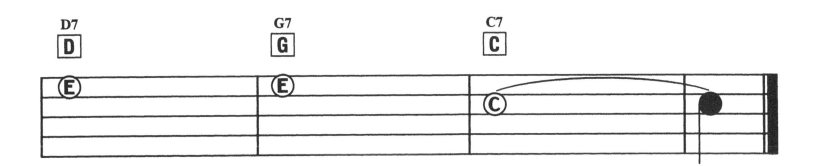

Chanson D'Amour
(Song Of Love)
(The Ra-Da-Da-Da-Da Song)

Registration 7
Rhythm: Swing or Jazz

Words and Music by
Wayne Shanklin

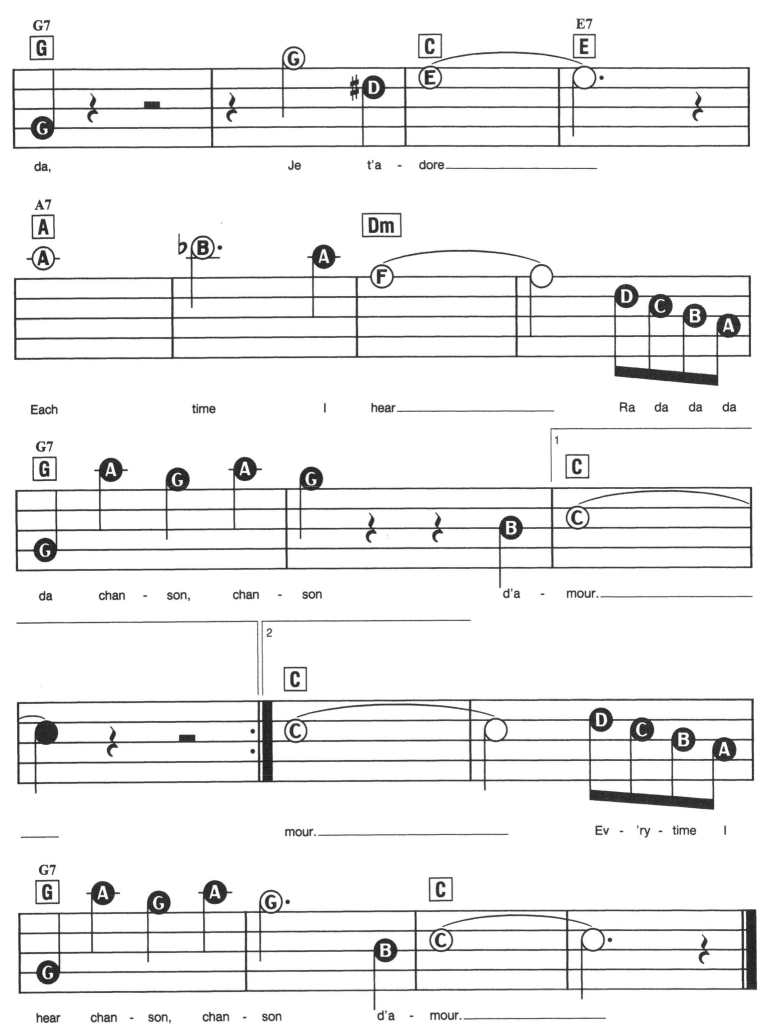

Cinco Robles
(Five Oaks)

Registration 4
Rhythm: Waltz

Words by Larry Sullivan
Music by Dorothy Wright

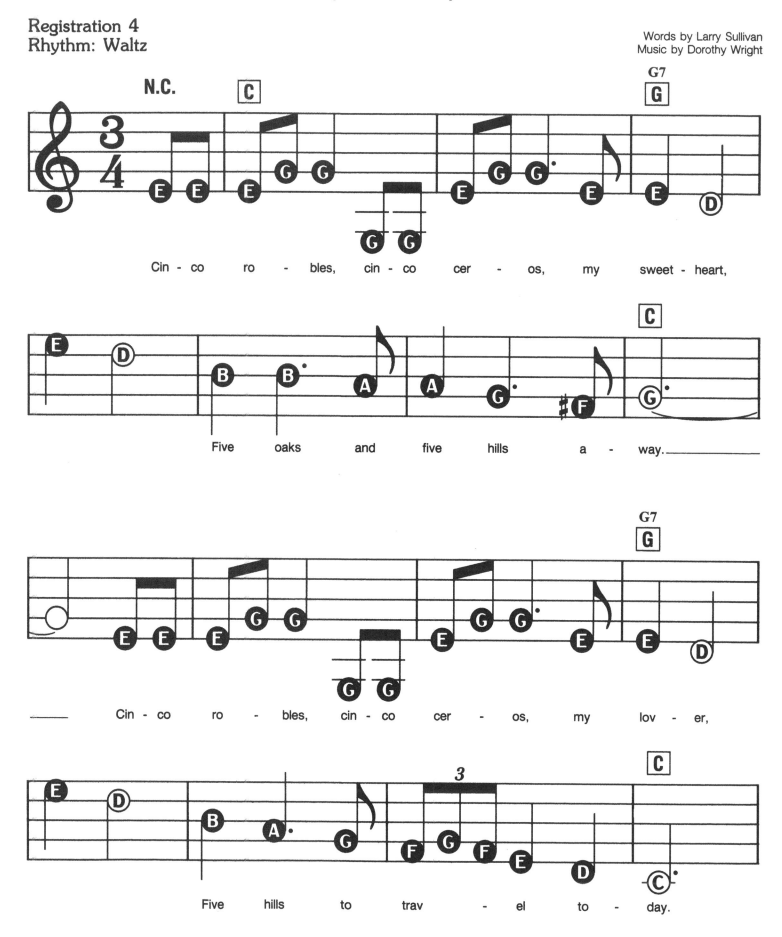

Cin - co ro - bles, cin - co cer - os, my sweet - heart,
Five oaks and five hills a - way.
Cin - co ro - bles, cin - co cer - os, my lov - er,
Five hills to trav - el to - day.

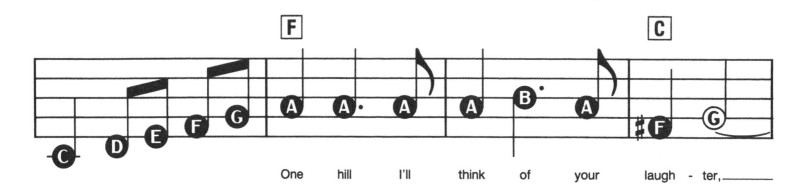

One hill I'll think of your laugh - ter,_____

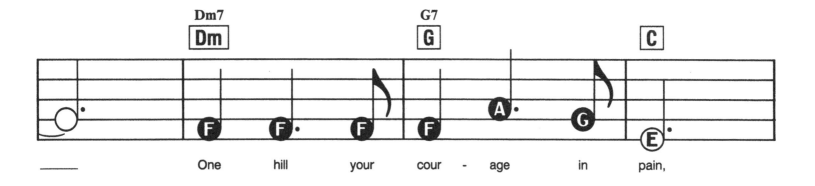

_____ One hill your cour - age in pain,

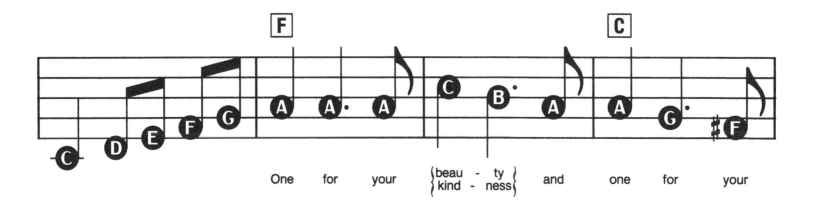

One for your {beau - ty / kind - ness} and one for your

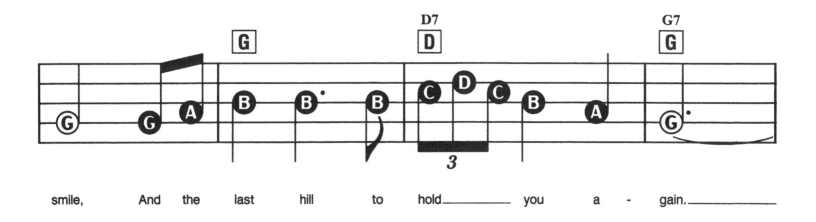

smile, And the last hill to hold_____ you a - gain._____

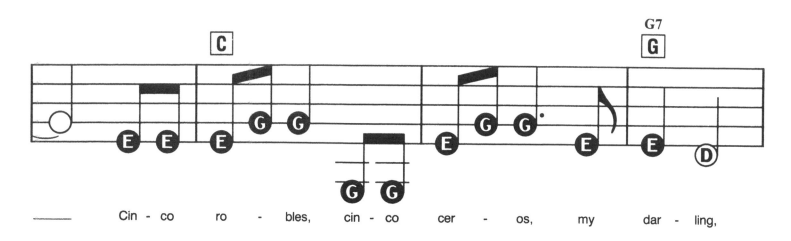

Cin - co ro - bles, cin - co cer - os, my dar - ling,

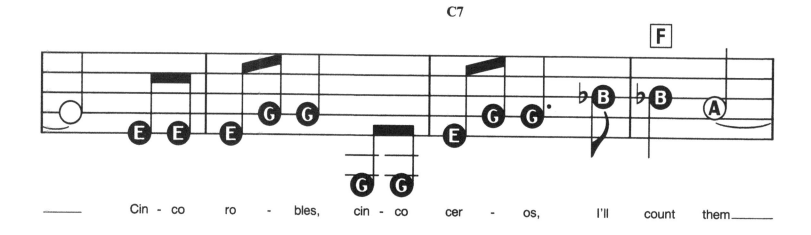

Five oaks and five hills a - part._____

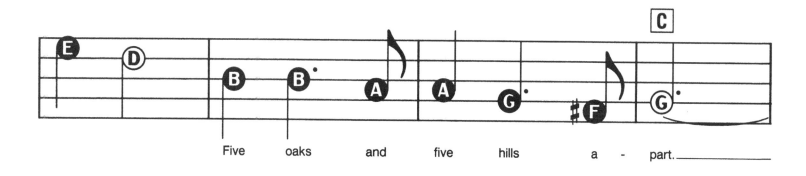

Cin - co ro - bles, cin - co cer - os, I'll count them_____

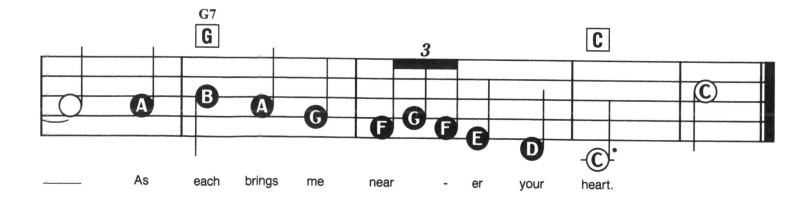

As each brings me near - er your heart.

Goin' Out Of My Head

Registration 7
Rhythm: Latin or Beguine

Words and Music by
Teddy Randazzo and Bobby Weinstein

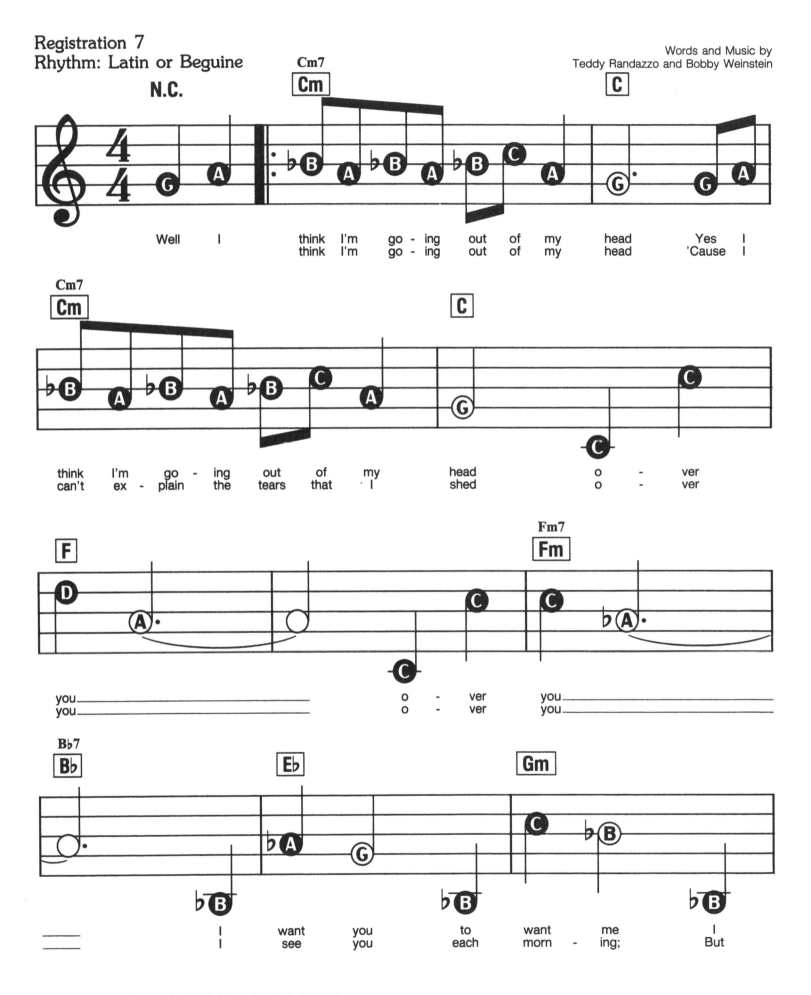

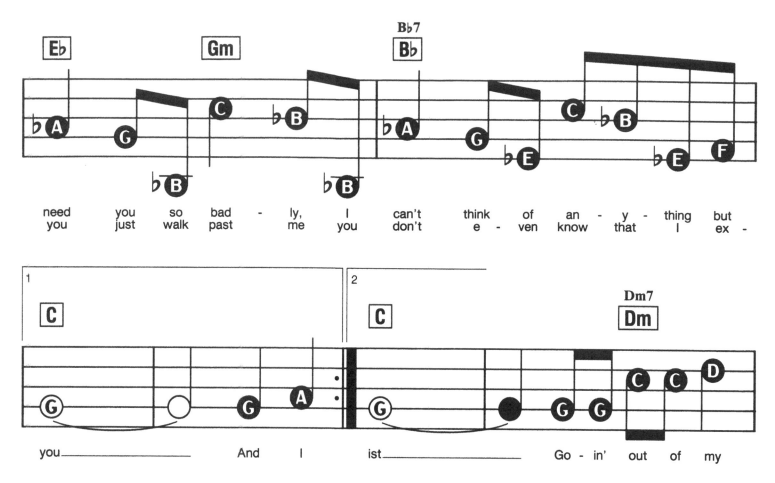

need you so bad - ly, I can't think of an - y - thing but
you just walk past me you don't e - ven know that I ex -

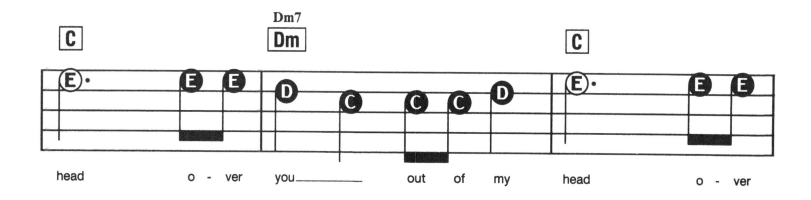

you_____ And I
ist_____ Go - in' out of my

head   o - ver you_____ out of my head   o - ver

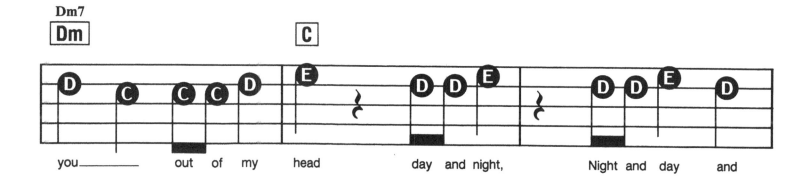

you_____ out of my head   day and night,   Night and day   and

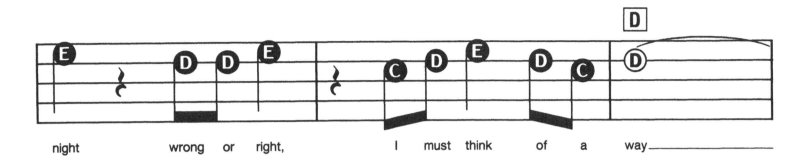

night   wrong   or   right,   I   must   think   of   a   way

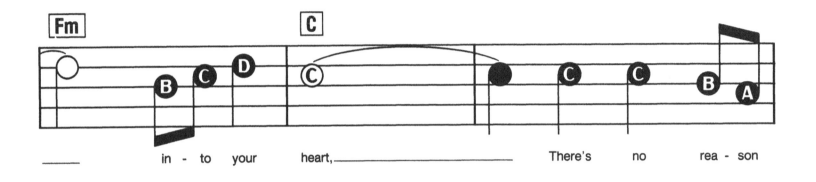

____   in - to   your   heart, _____ There's   no   rea - son

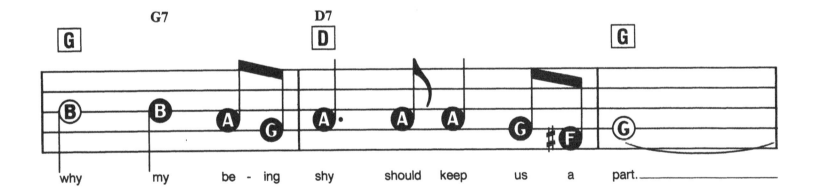

why   my   be - ing   shy   should   keep   us   a   part. ____

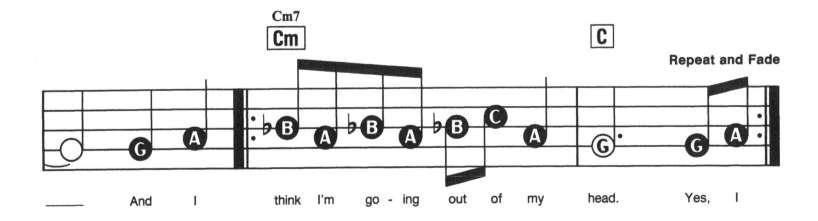

____   And   I   think   I'm   go - ing   out   of   my   head.   Yes,   I

Have You Looked Into Your Heart

Registration 3
Rhythm: Latin or Samba

Words and Music by Billy Barberis,
Teddy Randazzo and Bobby Weinstein

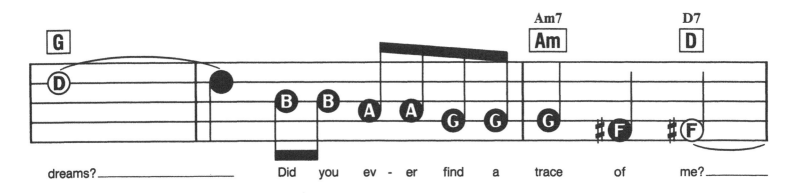

dreams?_____ Did you ev - er find a trace of me?_____

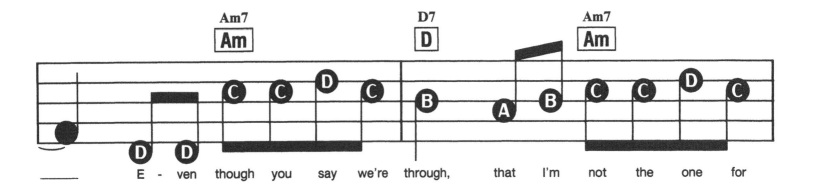

_____ E - ven though you say we're through, that I'm not the one for

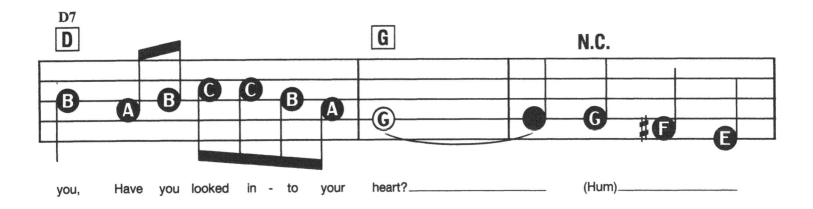

you, Have you looked in - to your heart?_____ (Hum)_____

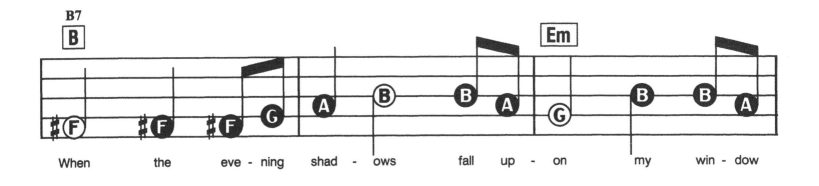

When the eve - ning shad - ows fall up - on my win - dow

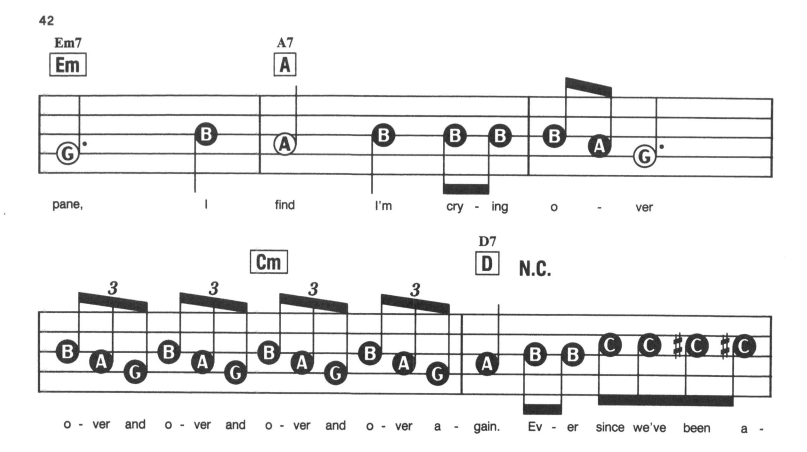

pane,   I   find   I'm   cry - ing o -   ver

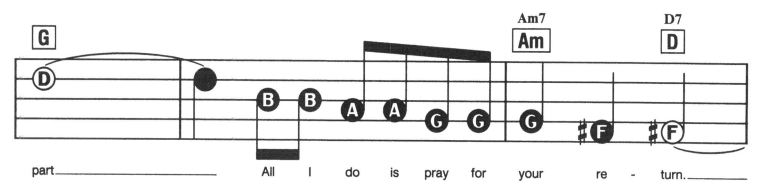

o - ver and o - ver and o - ver and o - ver a - gain. Ev - er since we've been a-

part_____ All I do is pray for your re - turn._____

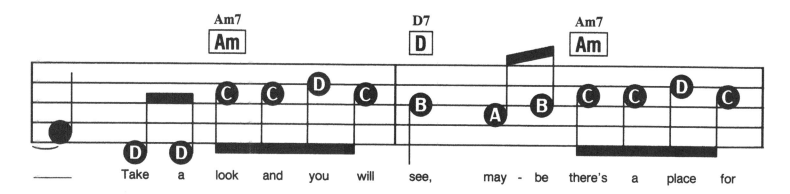

_____ Take a look and you will see, may - be there's a place for

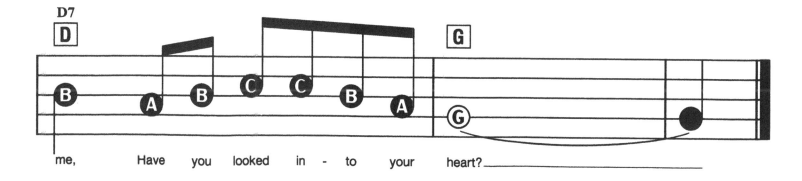

me,   Have you looked in - to your heart?_____

I Won't Dance

Words by Oscar Hammerstein & Otto Harbach
Screen Version by Dorothy Fields & Jimmy McHugh
Music by Jerome Kern

Registration 3
Rhythm: Fox Trot or Swing

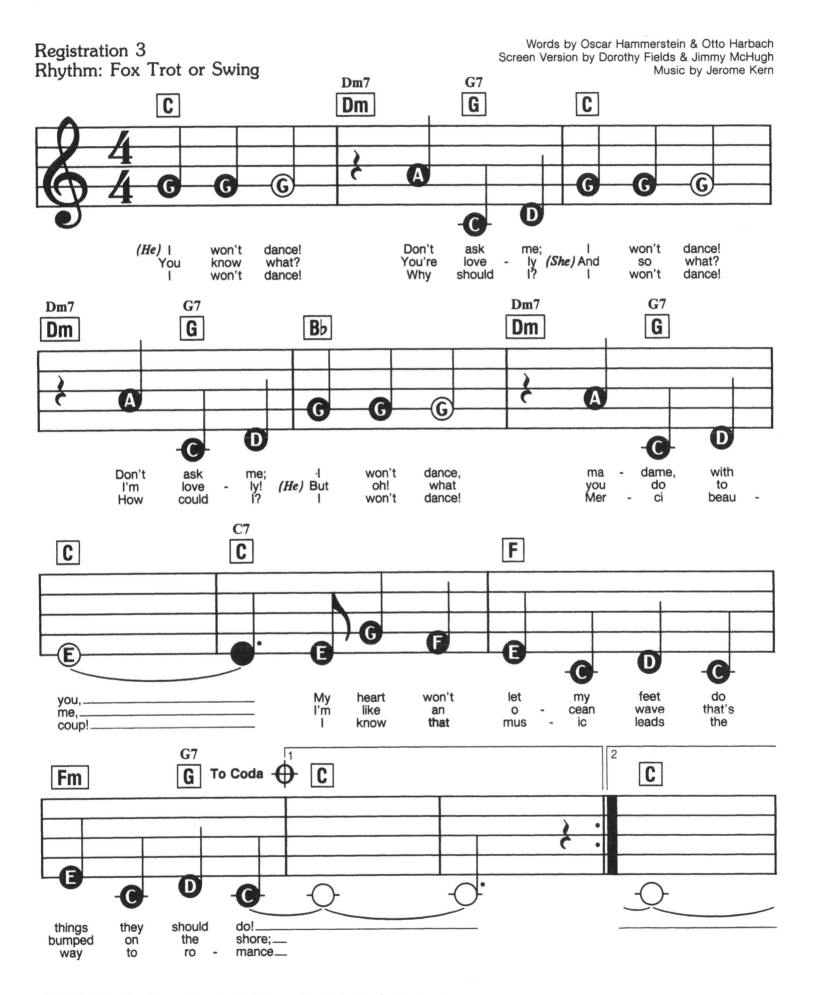

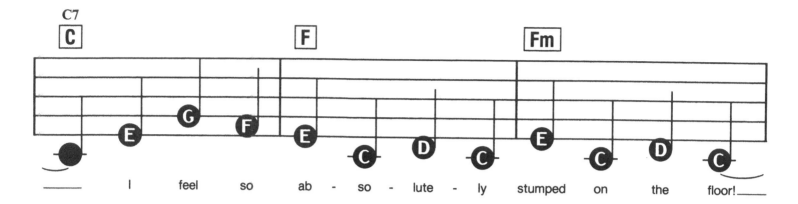

I feel so ab - so - lute - ly stumped on the floor!

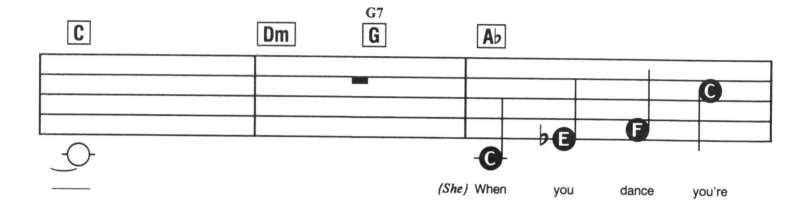

(She) When you dance you're

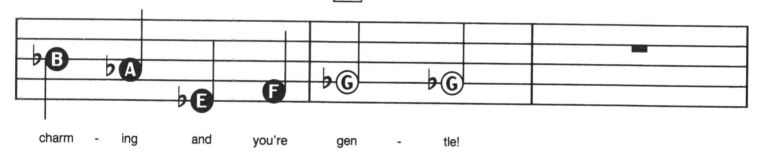

charm - ing and you're gen - tle!

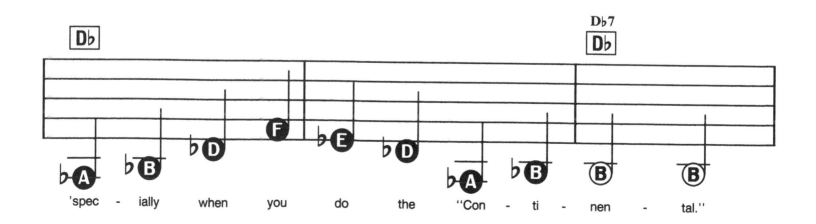

'spec - ially when you do the "Con - ti - nen - tal."

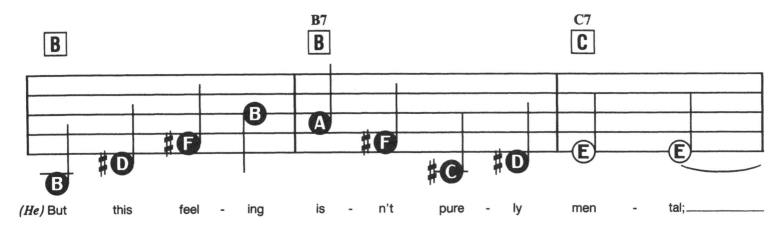

(He) But this feel - ing is - n't pure - ly men - tal;_____

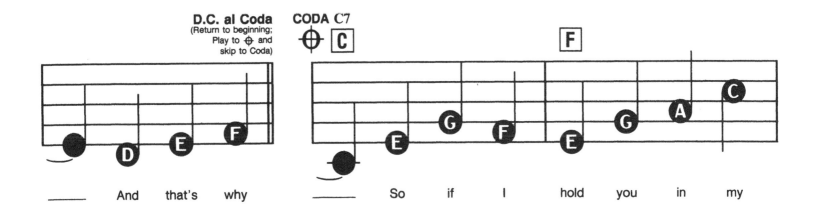

_____ For heav - en rest us,_____ I'm not as - bes - tos._____

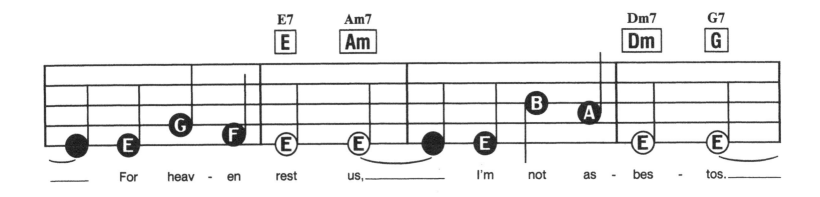

D.C. al Coda
(Return to beginning;
Play to ✛ and
skip to Coda)

CODA C7

_____ And that's why

_____ So if I hold you in my

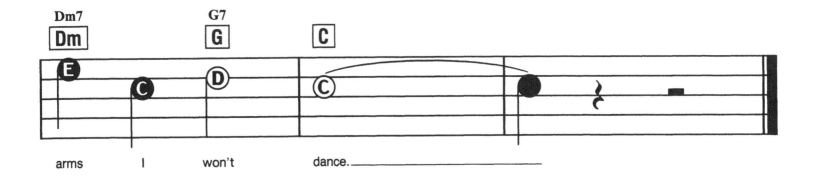

arms I won't dance._____

I Want A Girl
(Just Like The Girl That Married Dear Old Dad)

Registration 2
Rhythm: Swing or Jazz

By Will Dillon
and Harry Von Tilzer

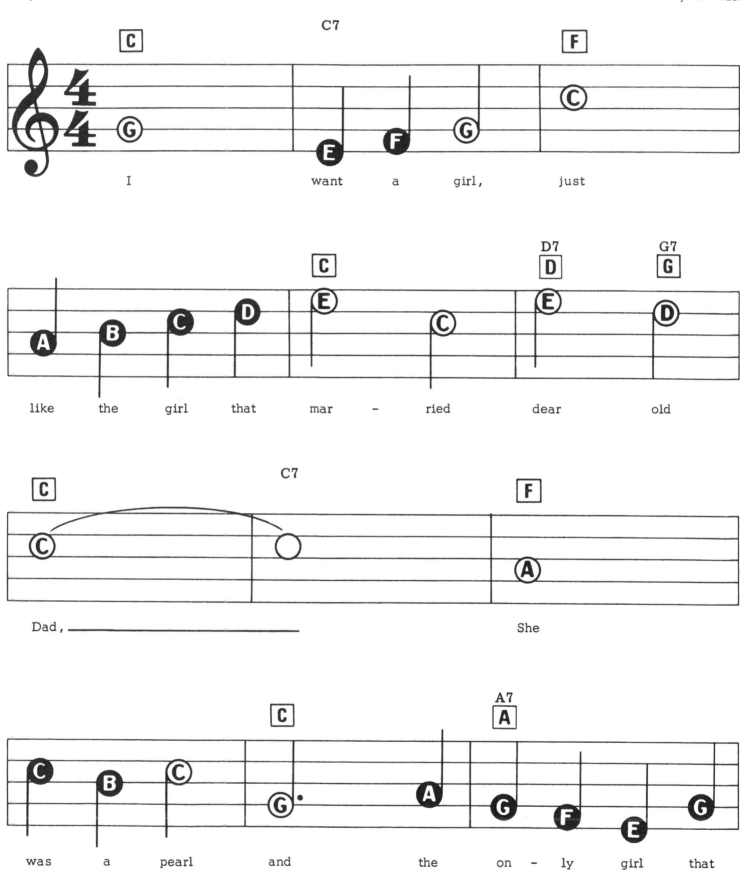

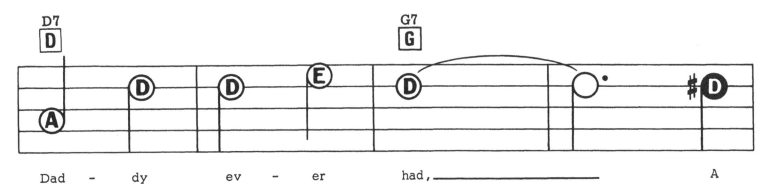

Dad - dy ev - er had, _____ A

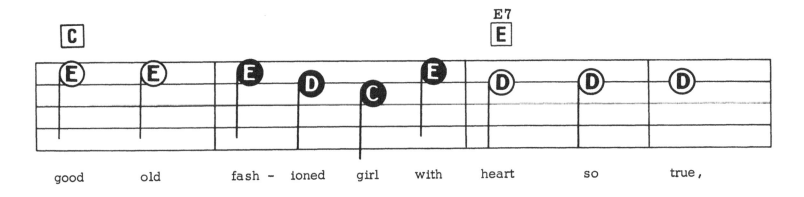

good old fash - ioned girl with heart so true,

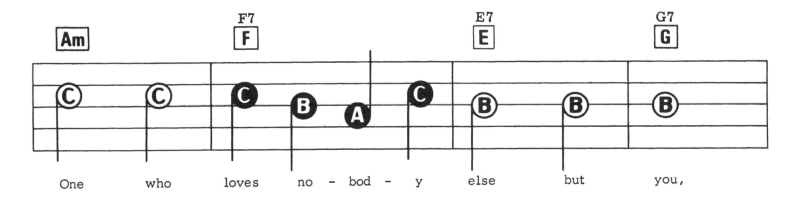

One who loves no - bod - y else but you,

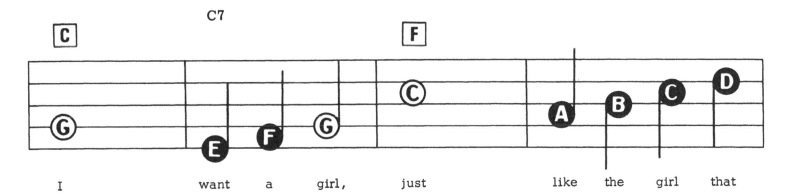

I want a girl, just like the girl that

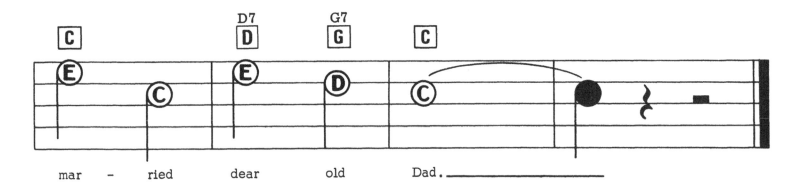

mar - ried dear old Dad. _____

I Will Wait For You

Registration 9
Rhythm: Fox Trot or Swing

English Words by Norman Gimbel
Music by Michel Legrand

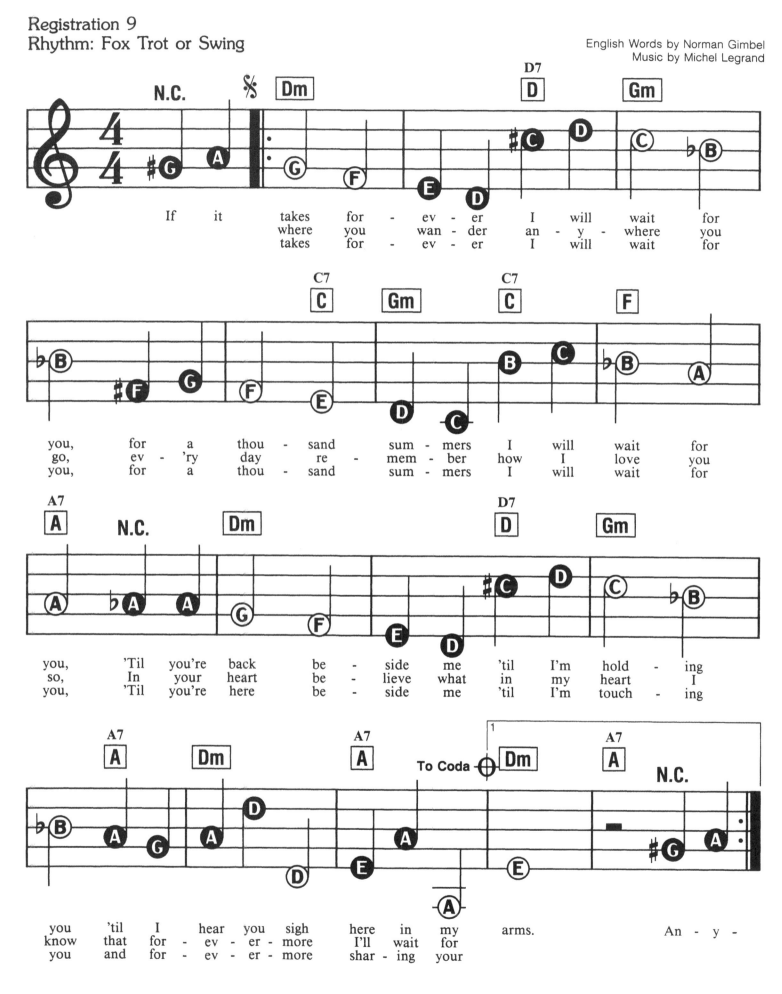

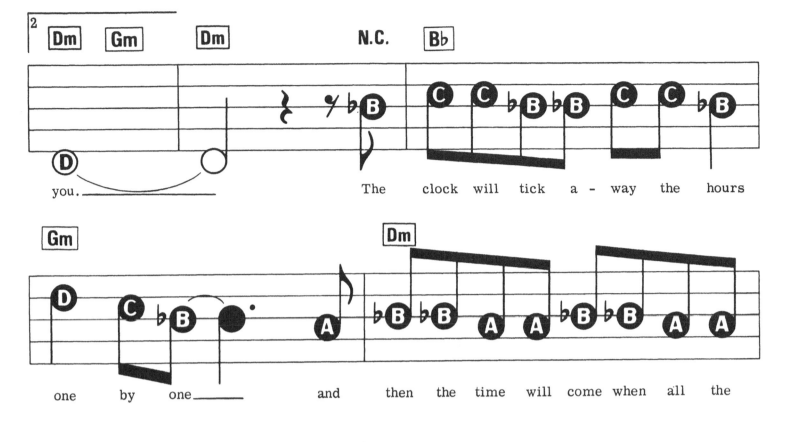

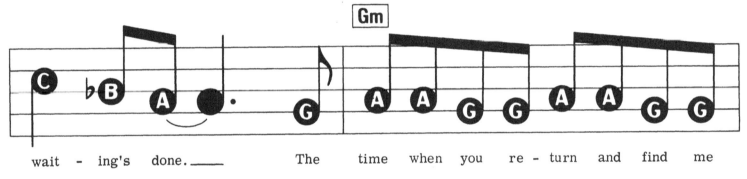

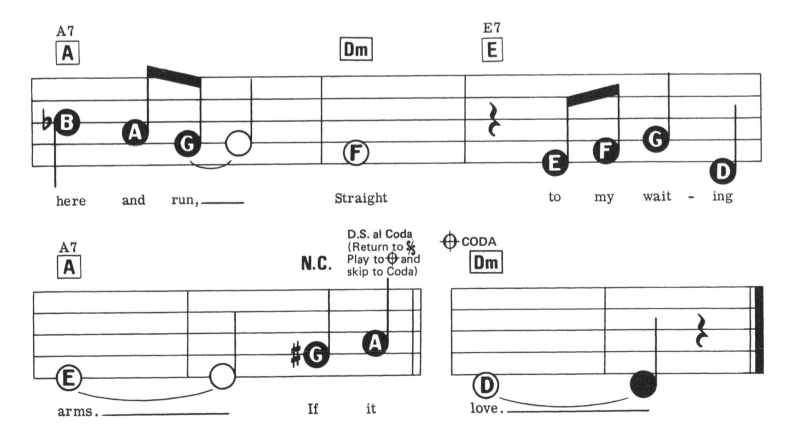

Isle Of Capri

Registration 8
Rhythm: Bossa Nova or Latin

Words by Jimmy Kennedy
Music by Will Grosz

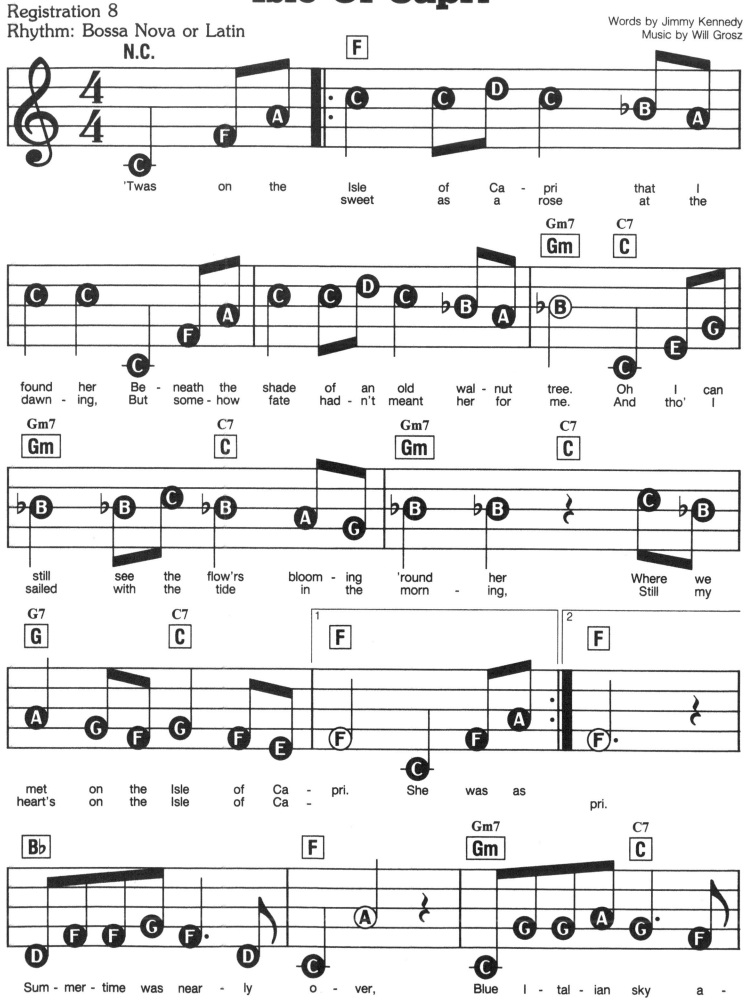

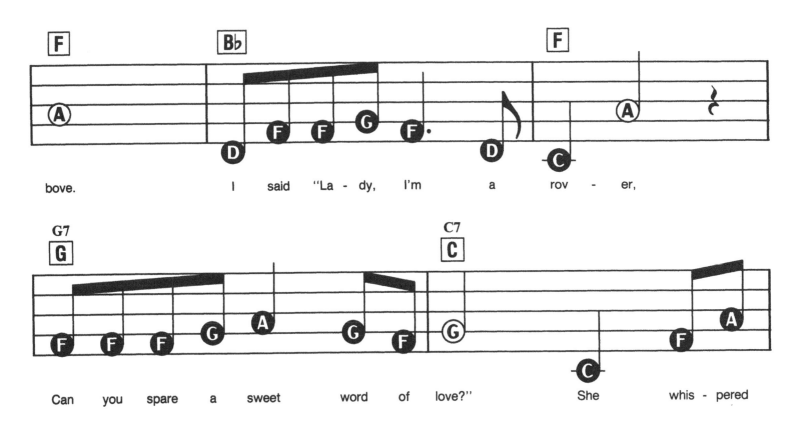

bove. I said "La - dy, I'm a rov - er,

Can you spare a sweet word of love?" She whis - pered

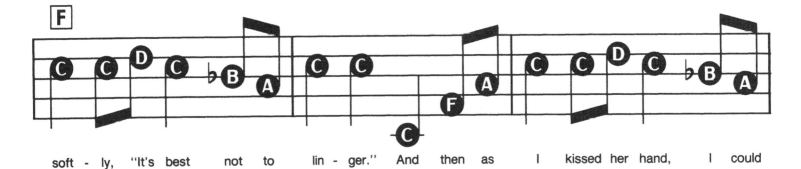

soft - ly, "It's best not to lin - ger." And then as I kissed her hand, I could

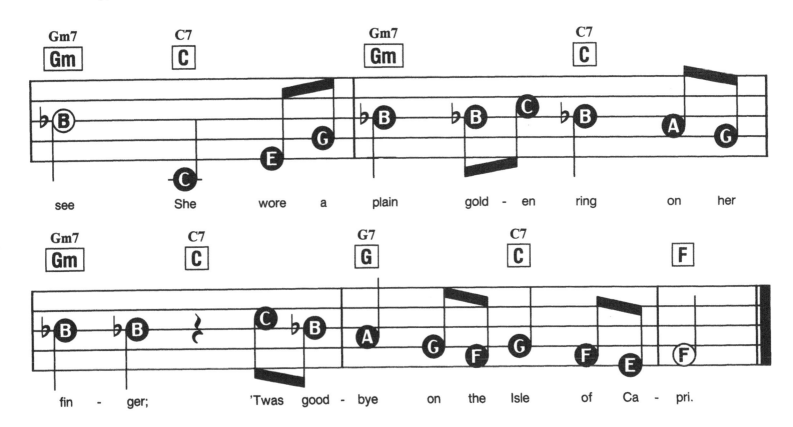

see She wore a plain gold - en ring on her

fin - ger; 'Twas good - bye on the Isle of Ca - pri.

La Vie En Rose

Registration 10
Rhythm: Ballad or Slow Rock

Original French Words by Edith Piaf
English Words by Mack David
Music by Louiguy

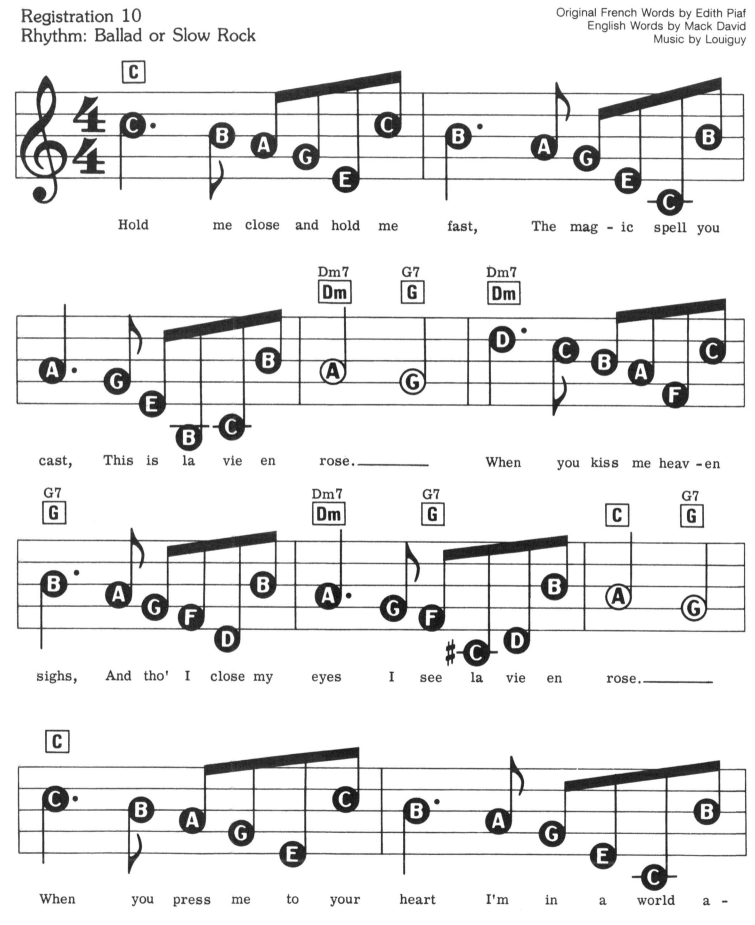

Hold me close and hold me fast, The mag - ic spell you

cast, This is la vie en rose._____ When you kiss me heav - en

sighs, And tho' I close my eyes I see la vie en rose._____

When you press me to your heart I'm in a world a -

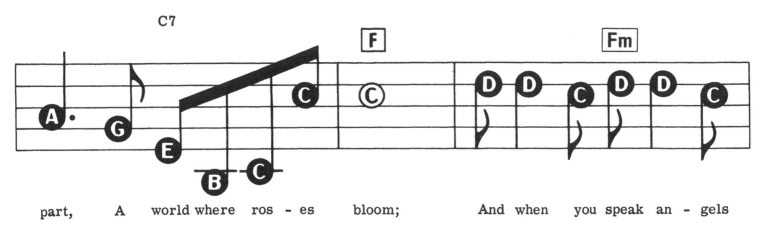

part, A world where ros - es bloom; And when you speak an - gels

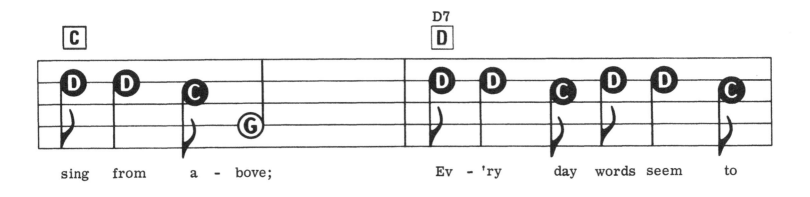

sing from a - bove; Ev - 'ry day words seem to

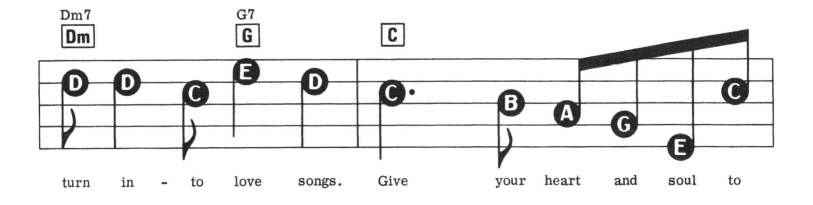

turn in - to love songs. Give your heart and soul to

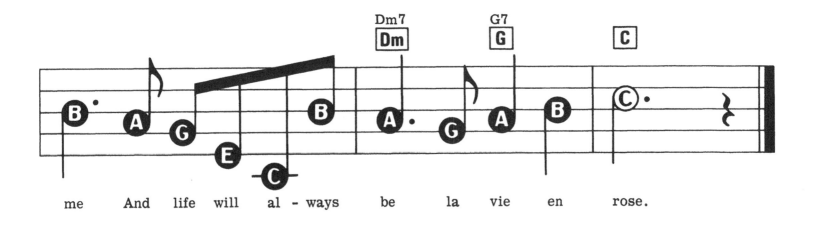

me And life will al - ways be la vie en rose.

Liechtensteiner Polka

Registration 5
Rhythm: Polka or March

Words and Music by
Ed Kotscher and R. Lindt

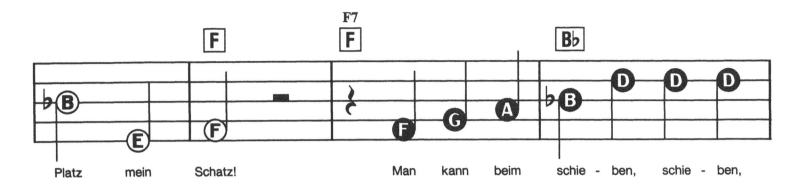

Platz mein Schatz! Man kann beim schie - ben, schie - ben,

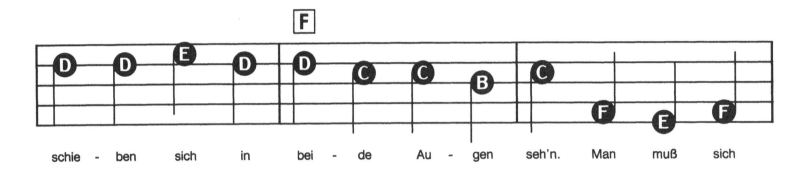

schie - ben sich in bei - de Au - gen seh'n. Man muß sich

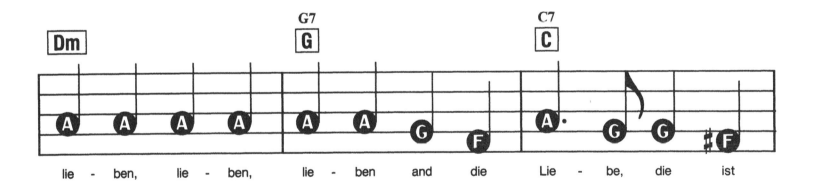

lie - ben, lie - ben, lie - ben and die Lie - be, die ist

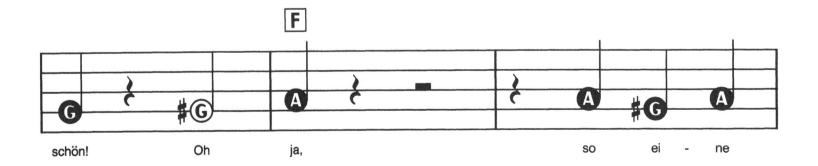

schön! Oh ja, so ei - ne

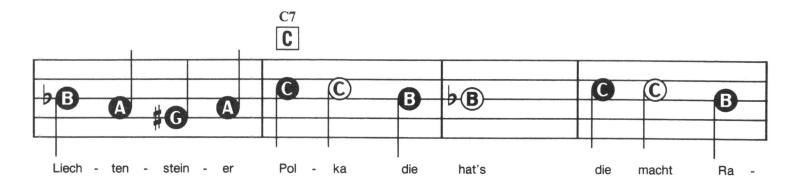

Liech - ten - stein - er Pol - ka die hat's die macht Ra -

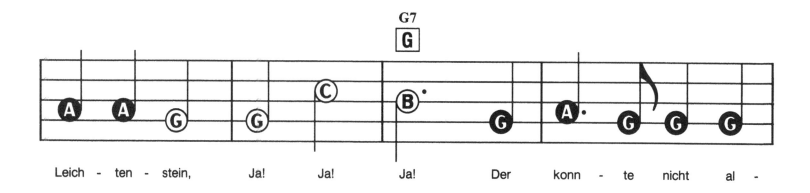

batz, mein Schatz! Der al - te Herr von

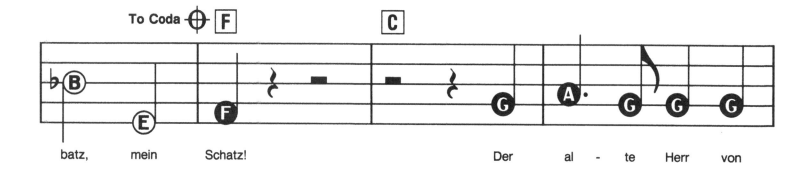

Leich - ten - stein, Ja! Ja! Ja! Der konn - te nicht al -

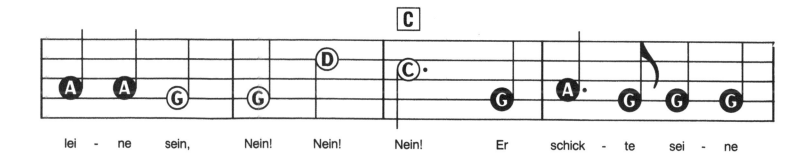

lei - ne sein, Nein! Nein! Nein! Er schick - te sei - ne

57

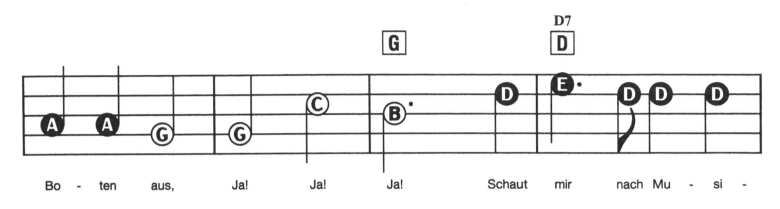

Bo - ten aus, Ja! Ja! Ja! Schaut mir nach Mu - si -

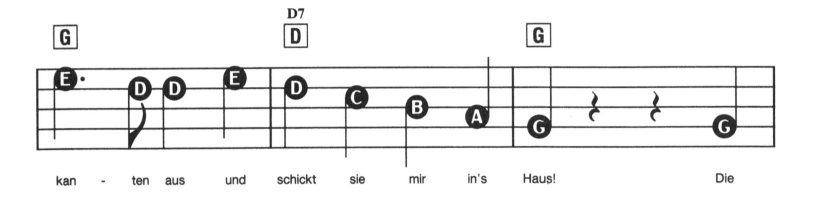

kan - ten aus und schickt sie mir in's Haus! Die

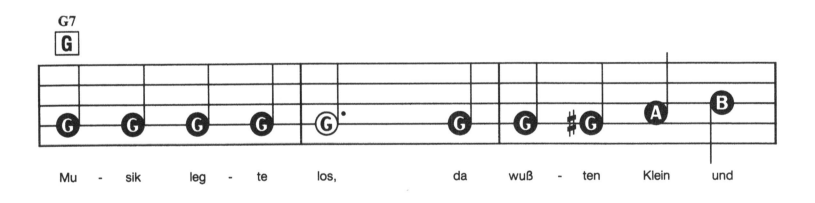

Mu - sik leg - te los, da wuß - ten Klein und

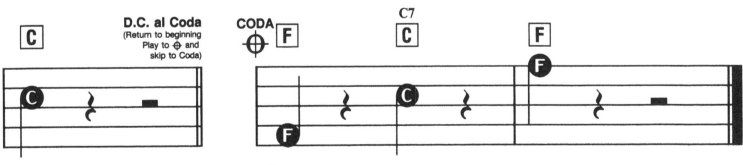

Groß: Schatz!

Lilli Marlene

Registration 9
Rhythm: Fox Trot or Ballad

German Lyric by Hans Leip
English Lyric by Tommie Connor
Music by Norbert Schultze

Little Girl Blue

Registration 4
Rhythm: Fox Trot or Ballad

Words by Lorenz Hart
Music by Richard Rodgers

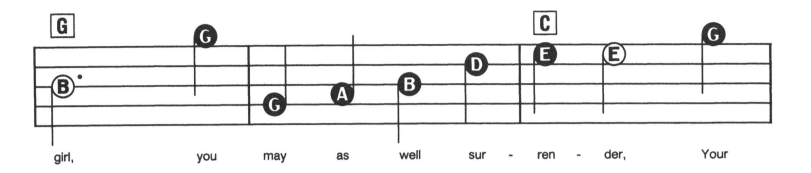

girl,   you   may   as   well   sur - ren - der,   Your

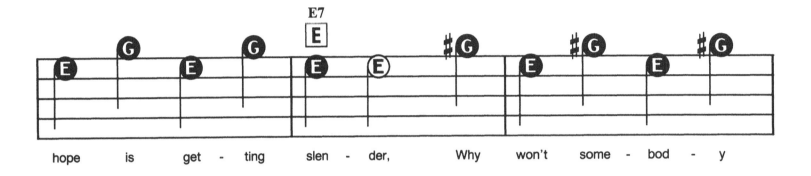

hope   is   get - ting   slen - der,   Why   won't   some - bod - y

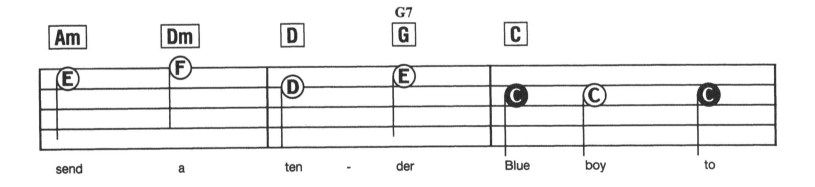

send   a   ten - der   Blue   boy   to

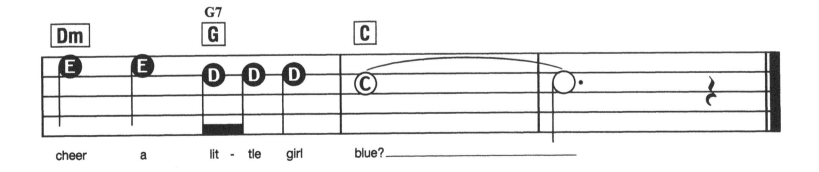

cheer   a   lit - tle   girl   blue?

Long Ago (And Far Away)

Registration 3
Rhythm: Ballad or Swing

Words by Ira Gershwin
Music by Jerome Kern

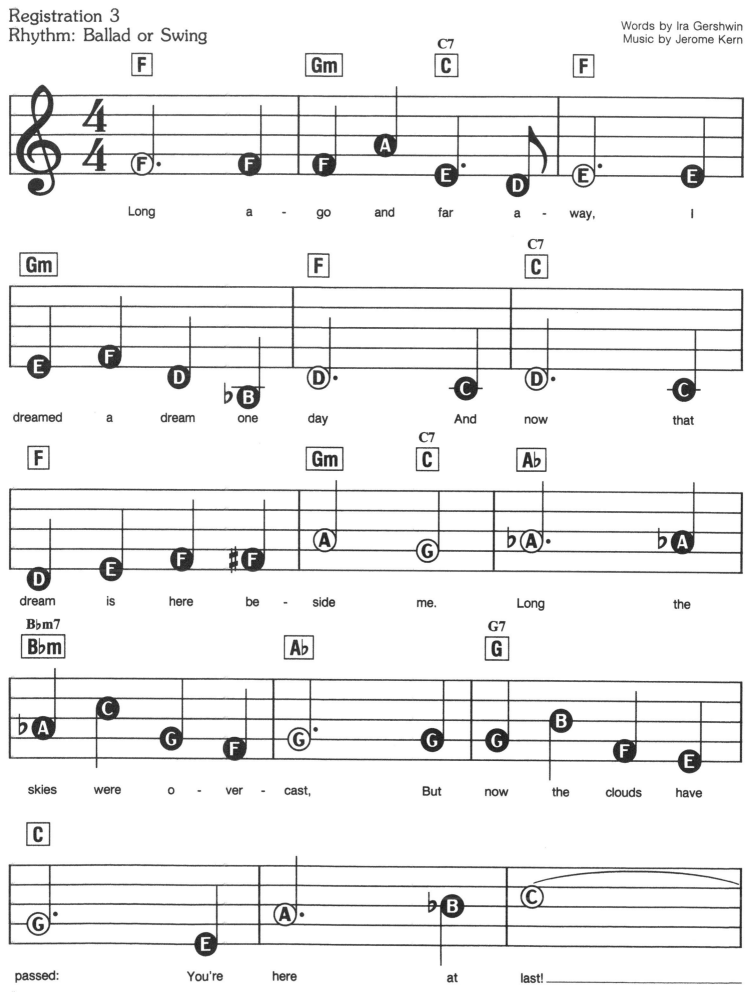

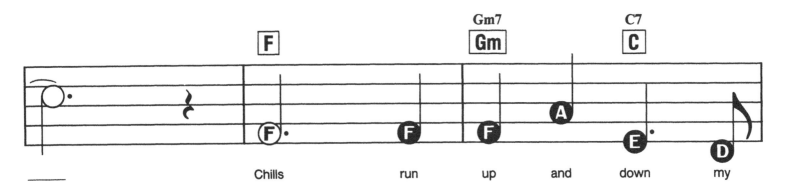

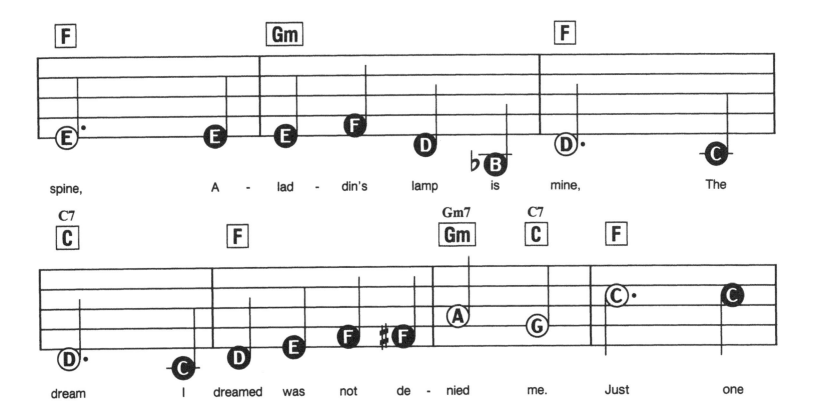

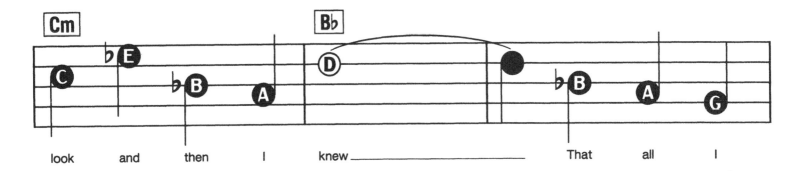

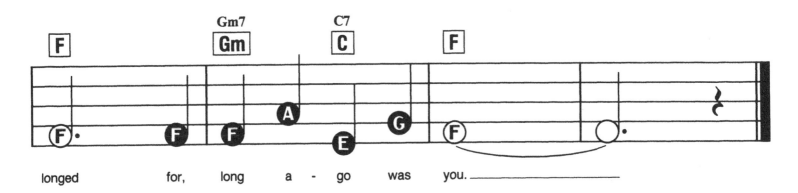

Look For The Silver Lining

Registration 2
Rhythm: Fox Trot or Swing

Words by Buddy DeSylva
Music by Jerome Kern

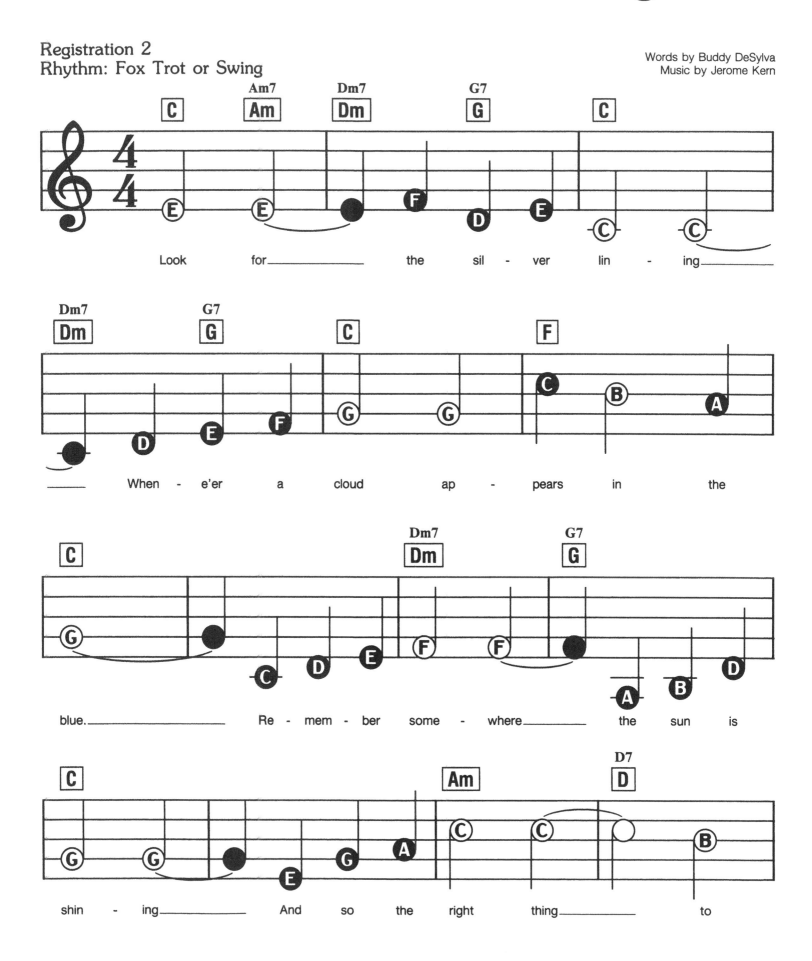

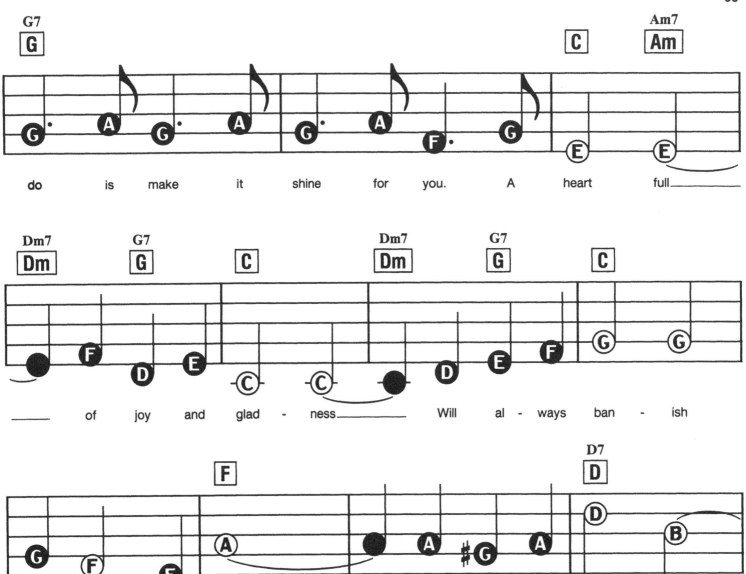

do is make it shine for you. A heart full____

____ of joy and glad - ness____ Will al - ways ban - ish

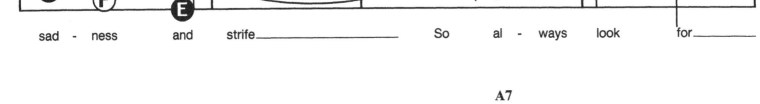

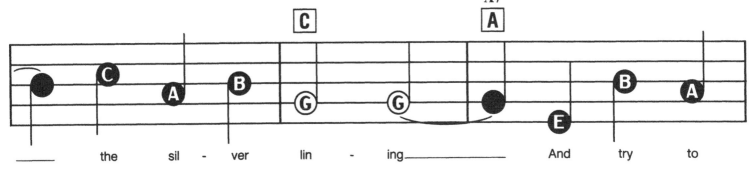

sad - ness and strife____ So al - ways look for____

____ the sil - ver lin - ing____ And try to

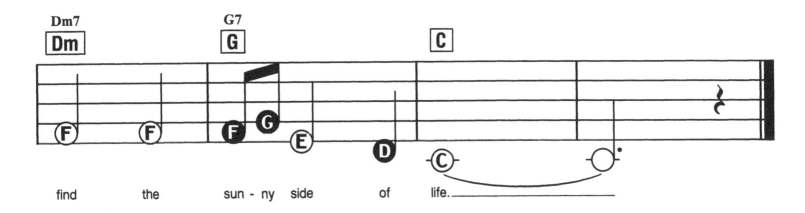

find the sun - ny side of life.____

Lovely To Look At

Registration 4
Rhythm: Ballad or Swing

Words by Dorothy Fields and Jimmy McHugh
Music by Jerome Kern

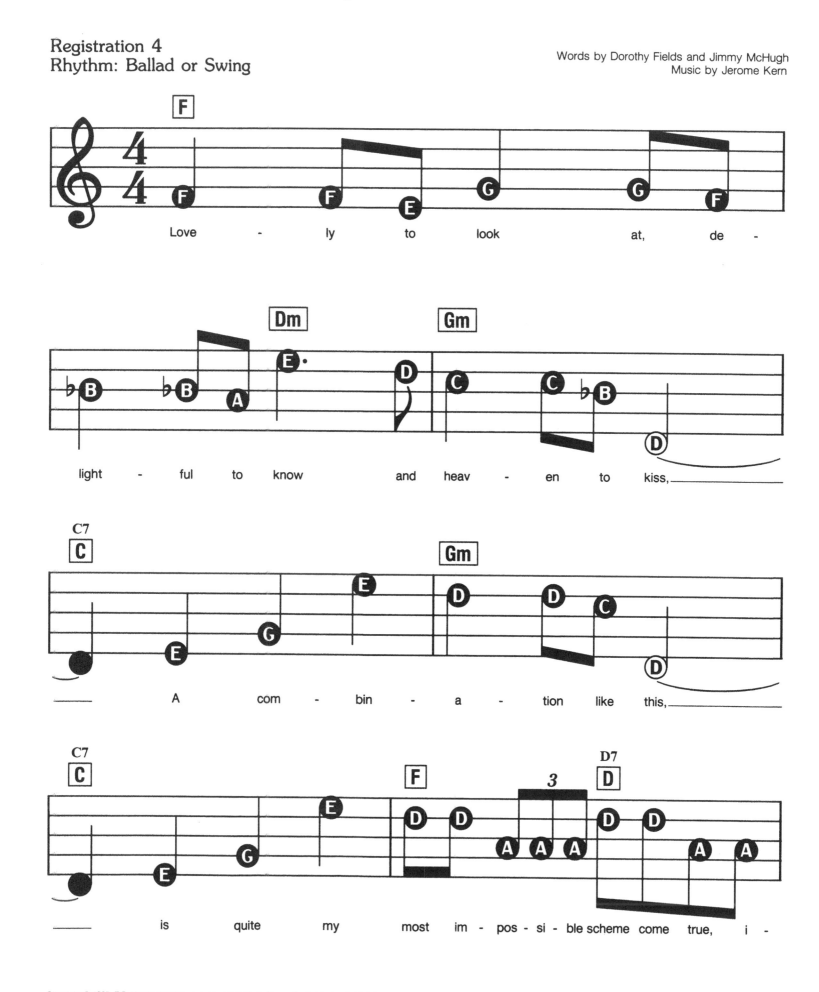

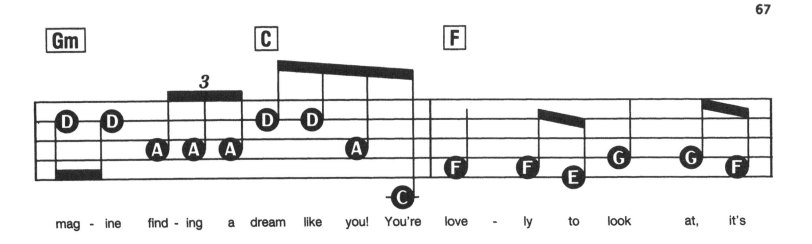

mag - ine find - ing a dream like you! You're love - ly to look at, it's

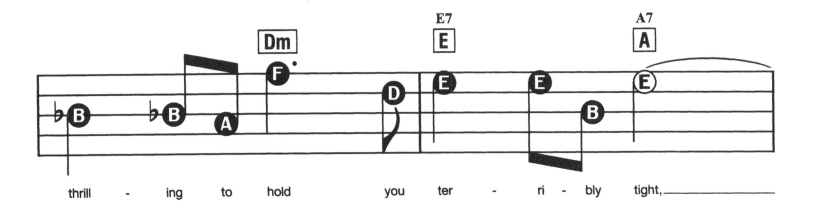

thrill - ing to hold you ter - ri - bly tight,

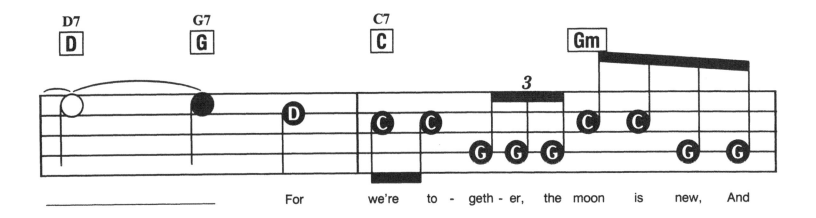

For we're to - geth - er, the moon is new, And

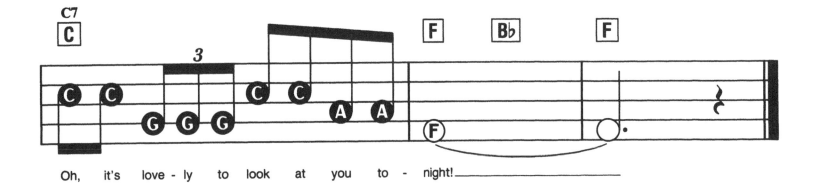

Oh, it's love - ly to look at you to - night!

Mack The Knife

(Aka "Moritat")

Registration 8
Rhythm: Swing

English Words by Marc Blitzstein
Original German Words by Bert Brecht
Music by Kurt Weill

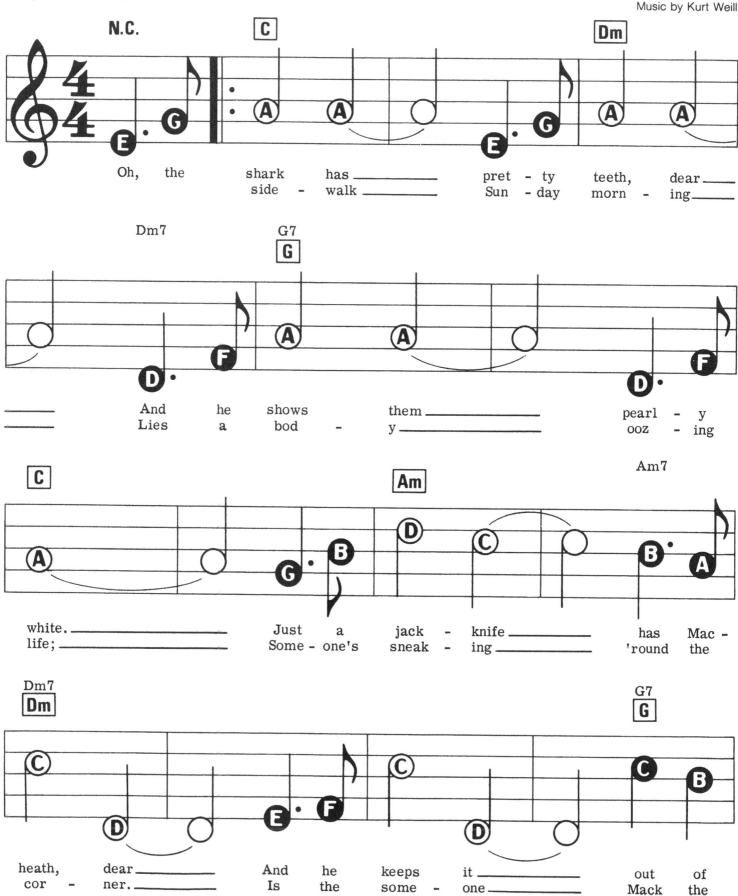

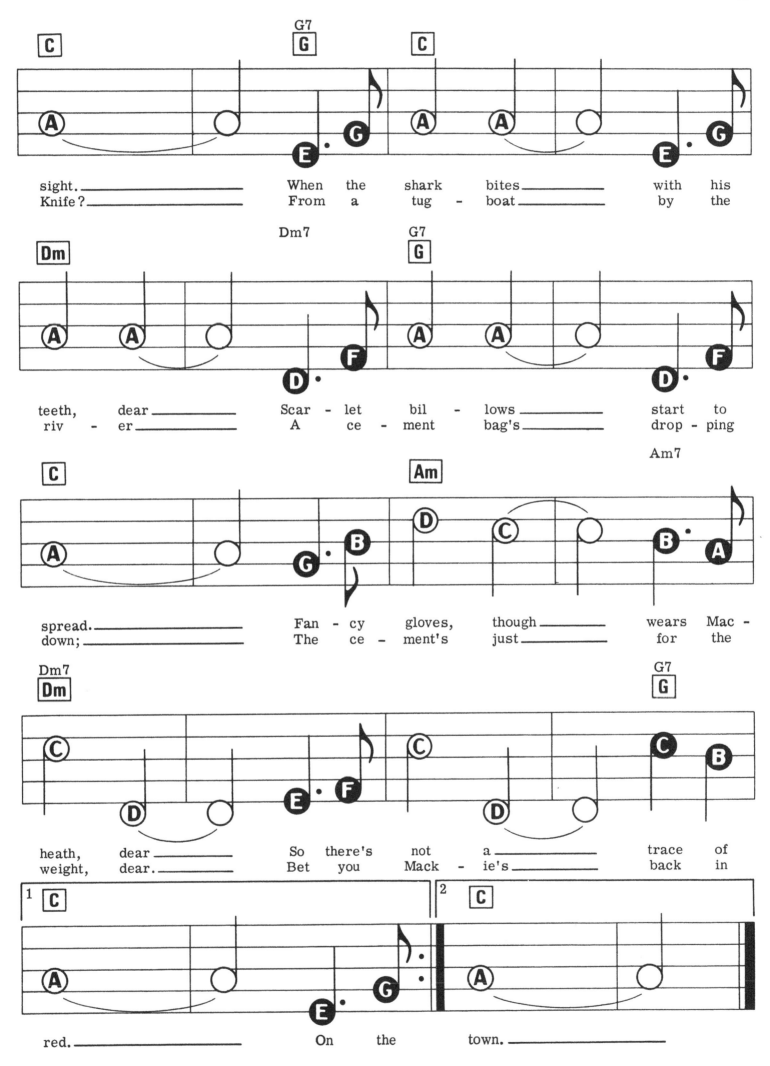

Make Believe

Registration 10
Rhythm: Fox Trot or Swing

Words by Oscar Hammerstein II
Music by Jerome Kern

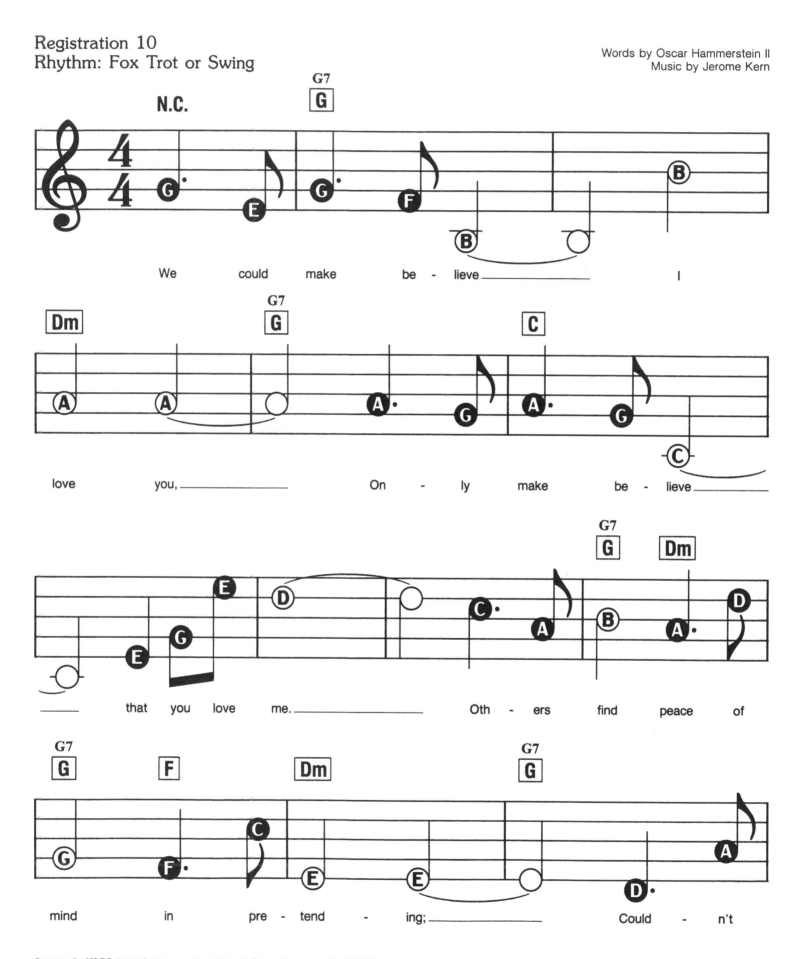

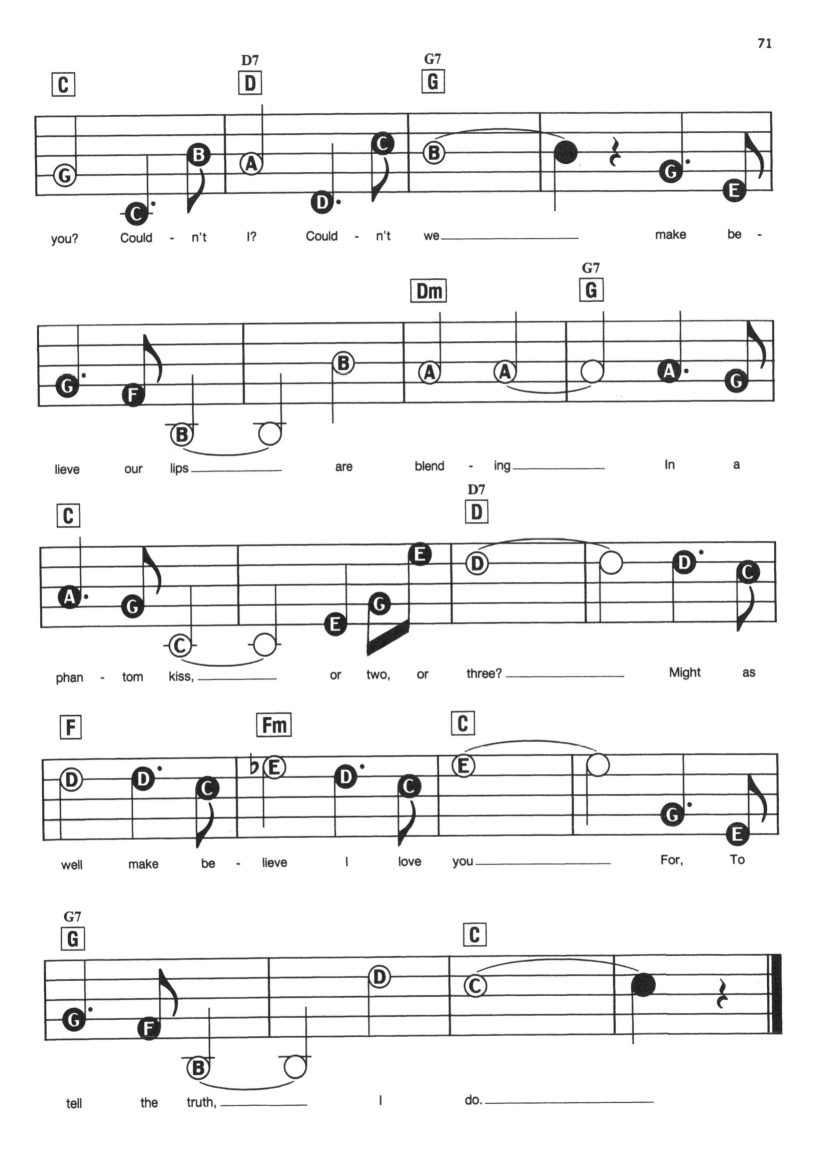

Mangos

Registration 7
Rhythm: Latin or Bossa Nova

By Dee Libbey and Sid Wayne

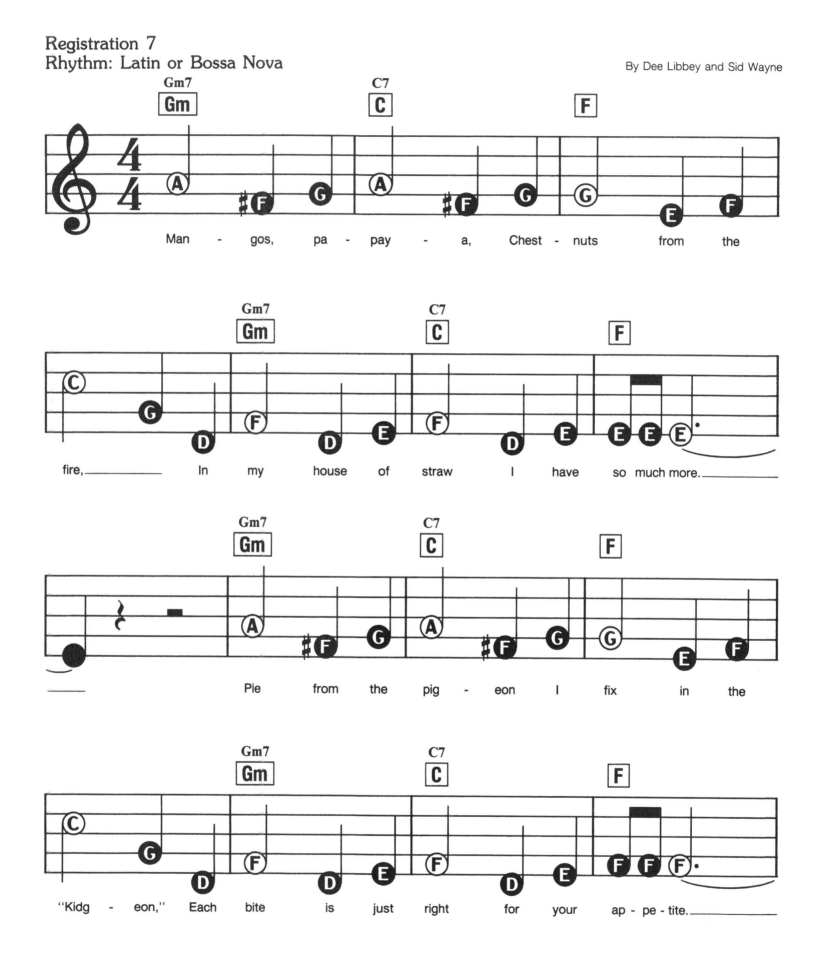

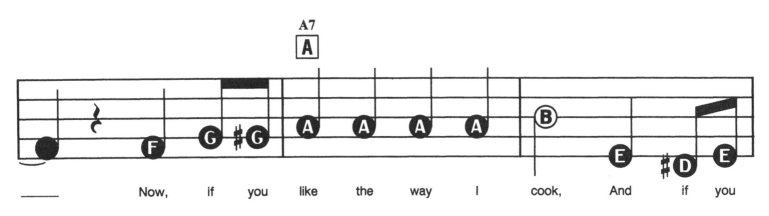

Now, if you like the way I cook, And if you

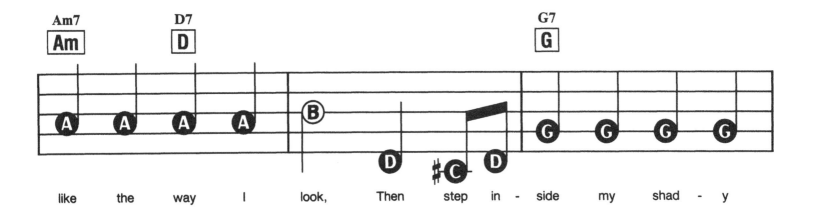

like the way I look, Then step in - side my shad - y

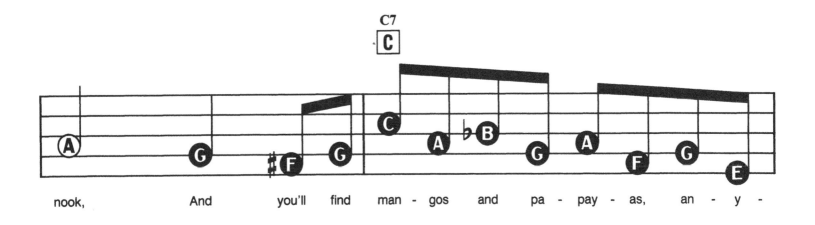

nook, And you'll find man - gos and pa - pay - as, an - y -

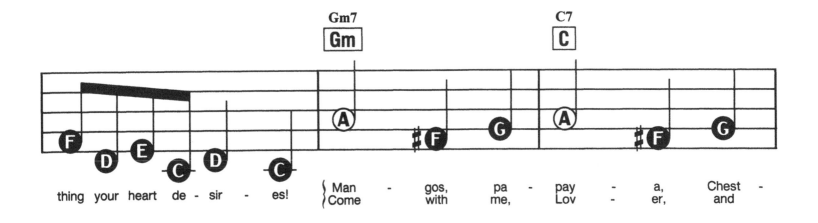

thing your heart de - sir - es!
{ Man - gos, pa - pay - a, Chest -
{ Come with me, Lov - er, and

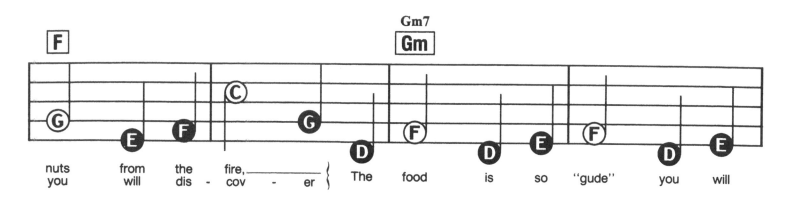

nuts from the fire,_____ { The food is so "gude" you will
you will dis - cov - er

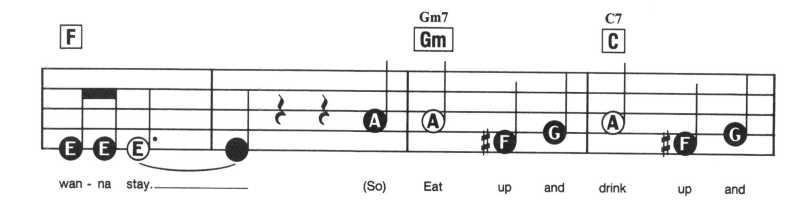

wan - na stay._____ (So) Eat up and drink up and

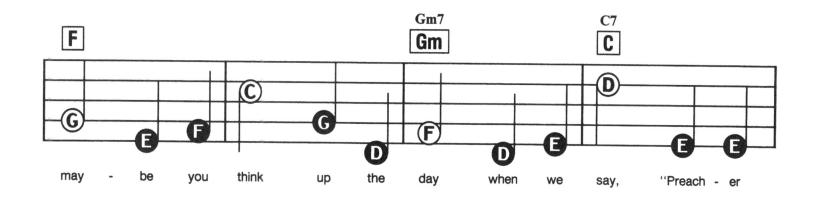

may - be you think up the day when we say, "Preach - er

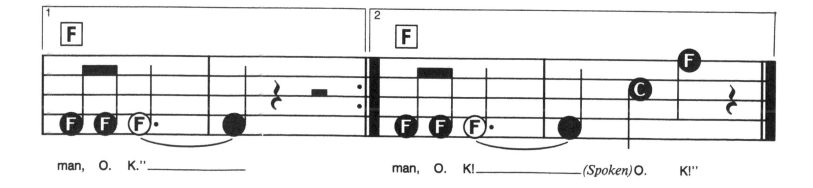

man, O. K."_____   man, O. K!_____(Spoken)O. K!"

The Most Beautiful Girl In The World

(From "JUMBO")

Registration 10
Rhythm: Waltz

Words by Lorenz Hart
Music by Richard Rodgers

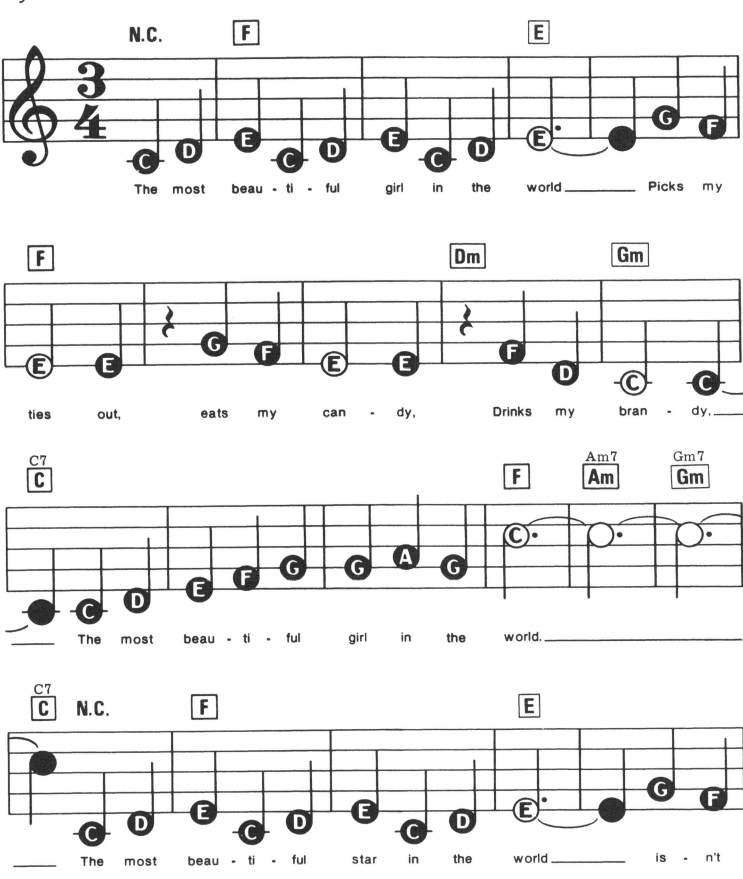

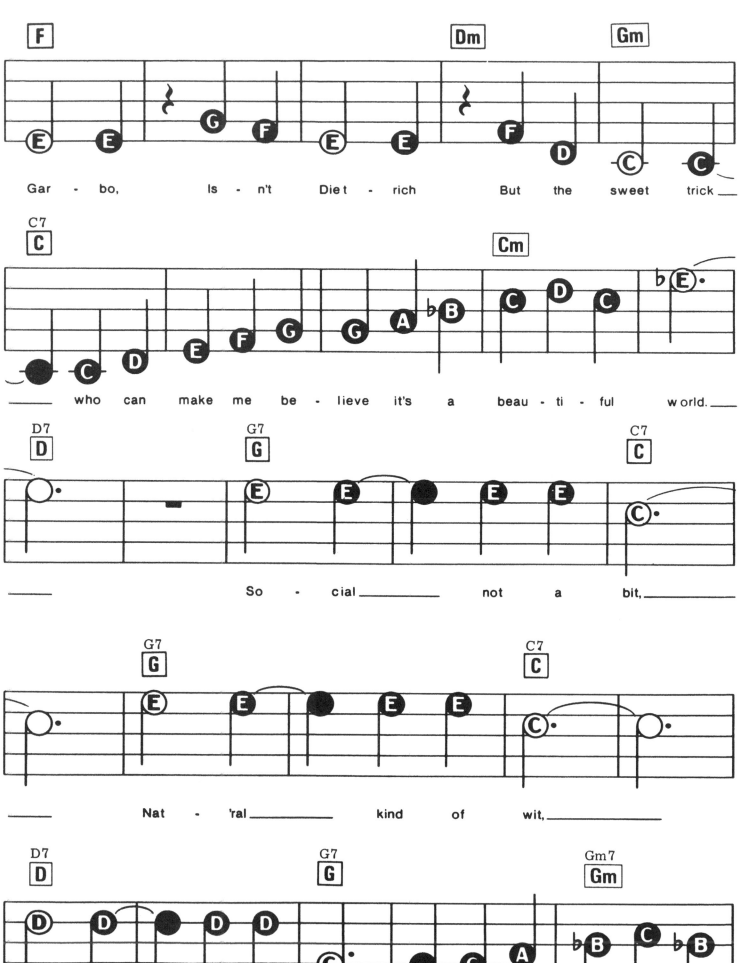

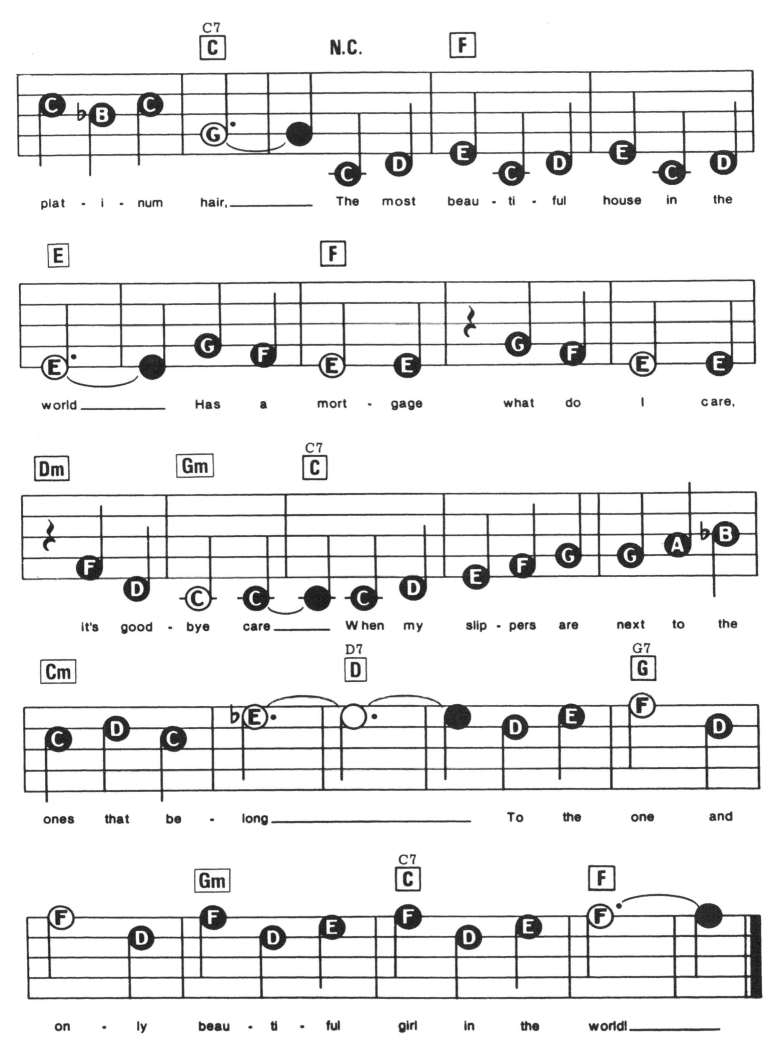

Moon Love
(Adapted from Tschaikowsky's Fifth Symphony, Second Movement)

Registration 5
Rhythm: Slow Rock or Ballad

By Mack David, Mac Davis
and Andre Kostelanetz

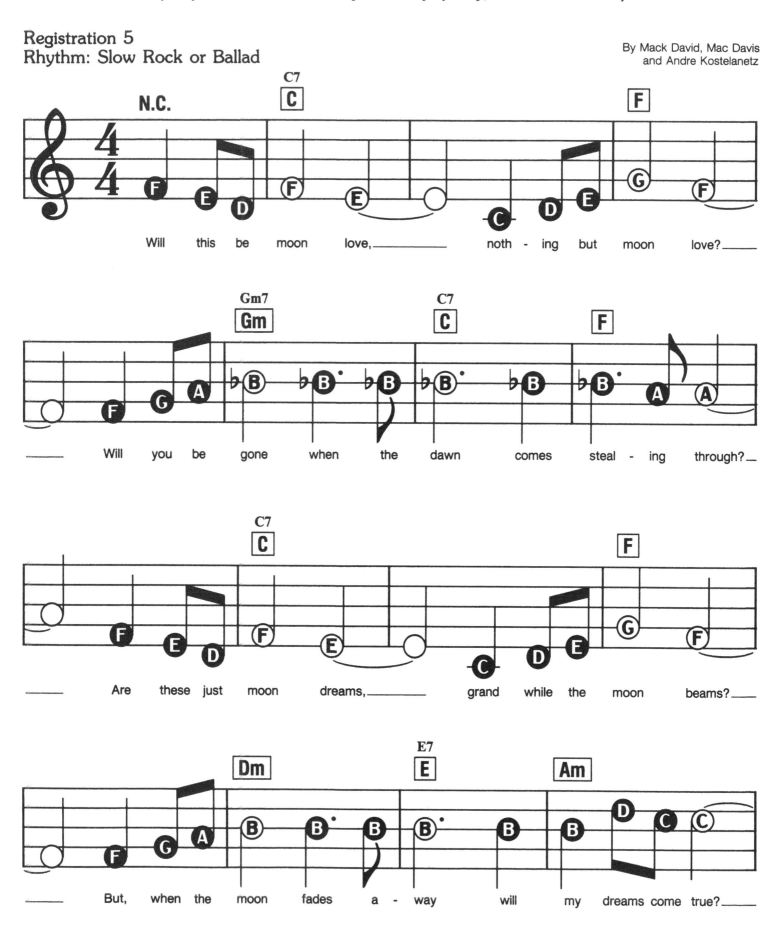

My Romance

(From "JUMBO")

Registration 5
Rhythm: Fox Trot or Ballad

Words by Lorenz Hart
Music by Richard Rodgers

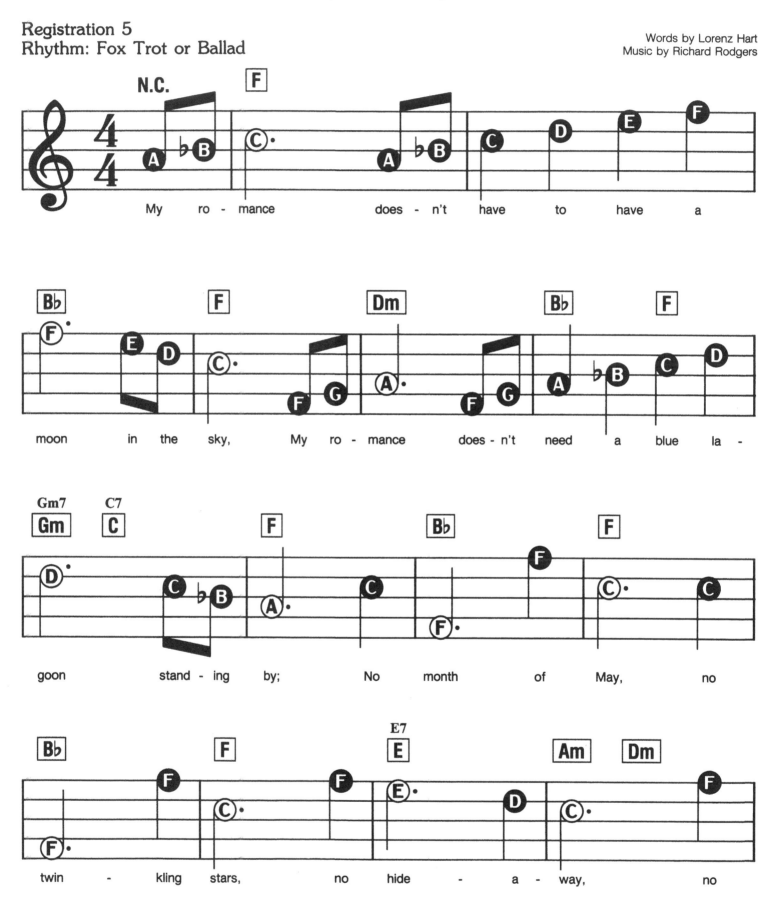

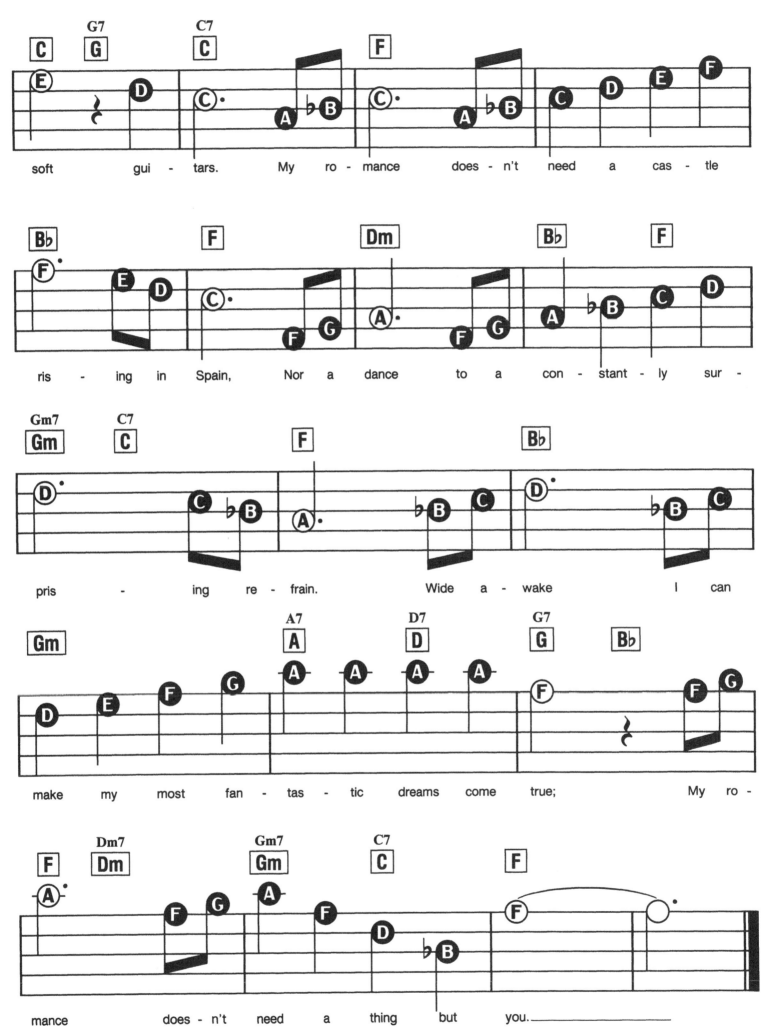

Ol' Man River

Registration 5
Rhythm: Ballad or Fox Trot

Words by Oscar Hammerstein II
Music by Jerome Kern

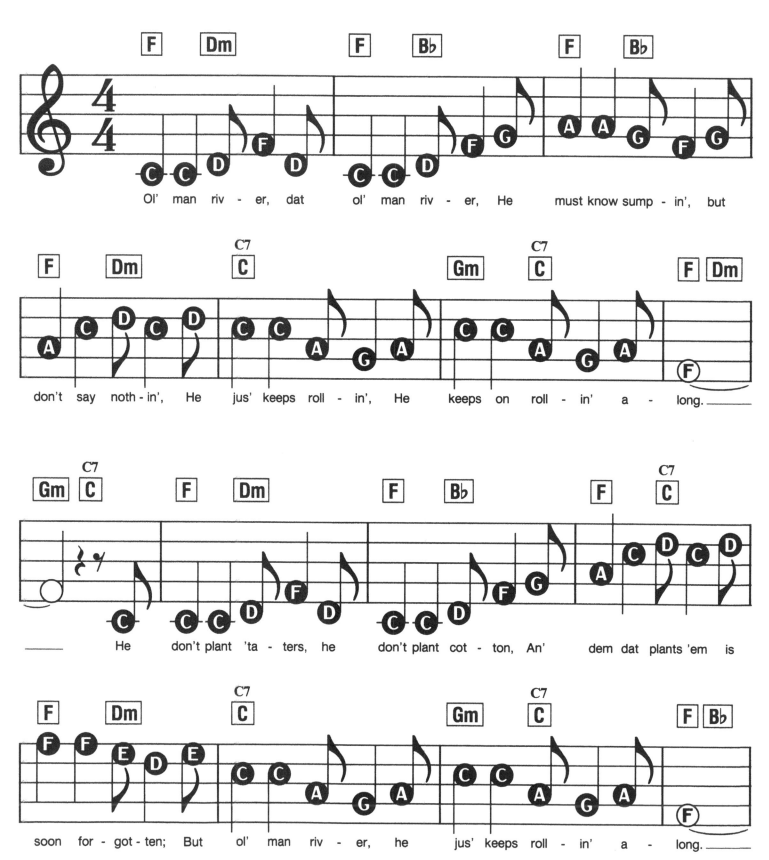

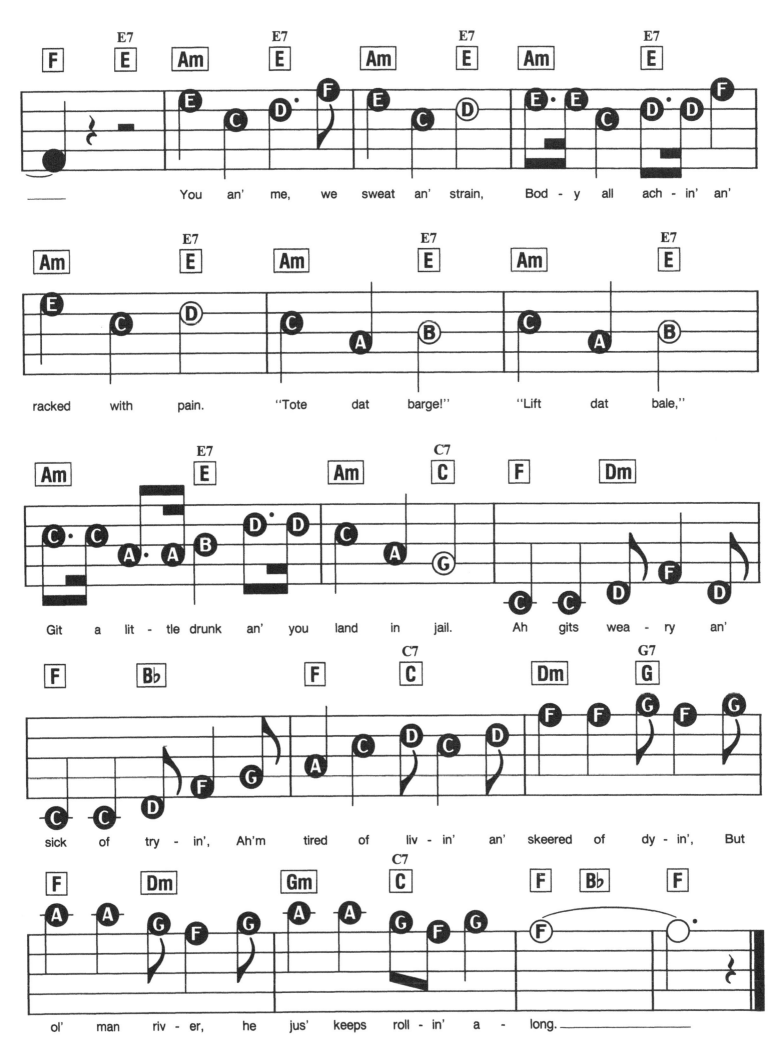

The Old Lamplighter

Registration 2
Rhythm: Swing or Jazz

Words by Charles Tobias
Music by Nat Simon

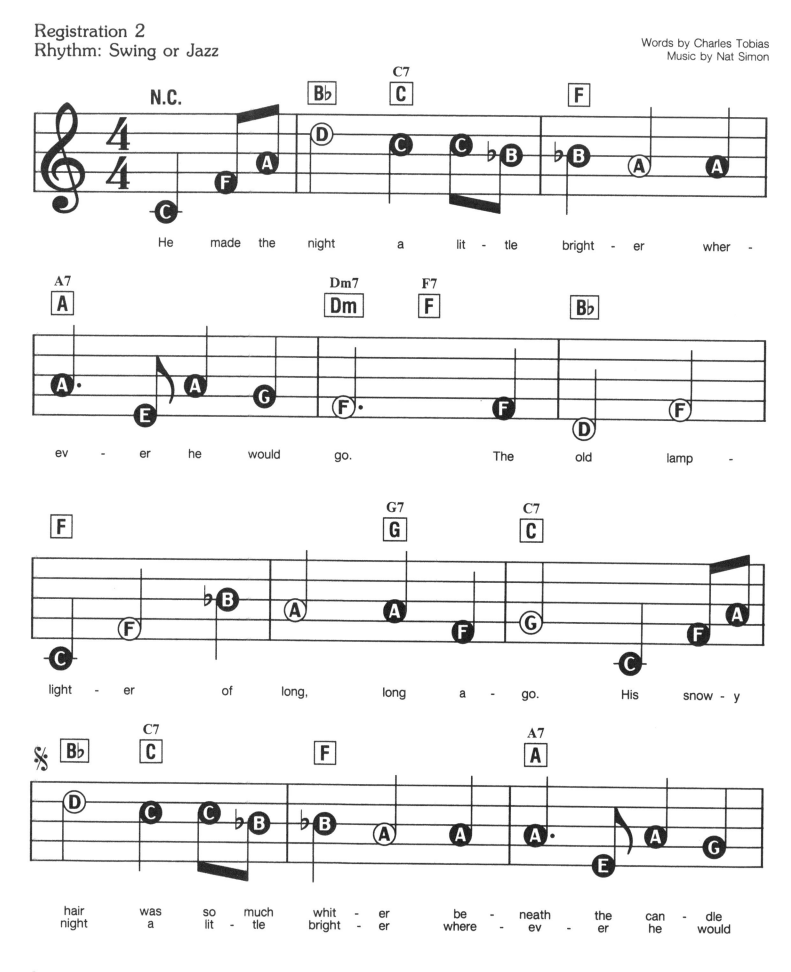

Orchids In The Moonlight

Registration 10
Rhythm: Latin or Tango

Words by Gus Kahn and Edward Eliscu
Music by Vincent Youmans

Em

E E #F G #F E
When or - chids bloom in the moon - light

C **Em**
C B

B7
B

B B C D C B #D
and lov - ers vow to be true,

A A B C B A
I still can dream in the

F#m7 **B7**
F#m **B**

E #D
moon - light

B B C D C B
Of one dear night that we knew.

Em
E

C **Em** **E7**
C **Em** **E**

C B

B B C D C B
They speak of tears and "Good

E E #F G #F E
When or - chids fade in the dawn - ing,

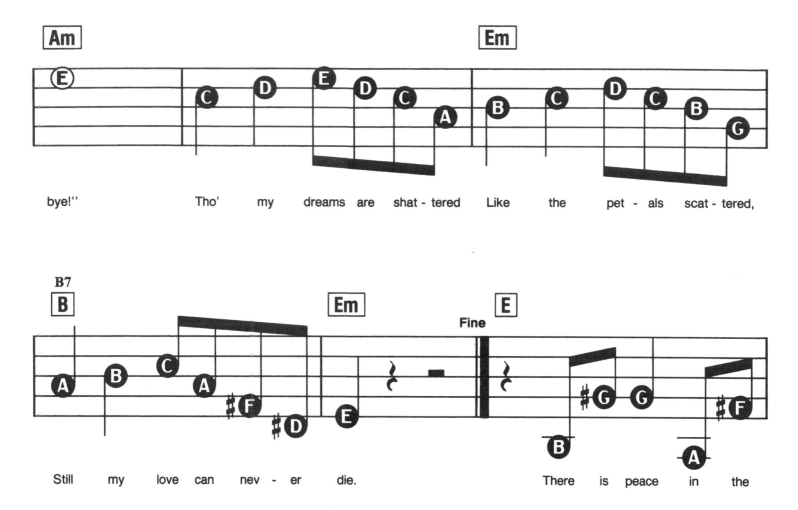

bye!''   Tho'   my   dreams are   shat - tered   Like   the   pet - als   scat - tered,

Still   my   love   can   nev - er   die.   There   is   peace   in   the

twi - light_____   when   the   day   is   thru,_____

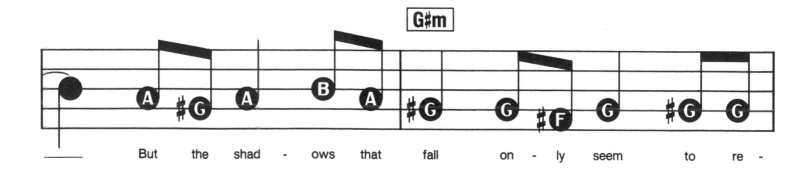

But   the   shad - ows   that   fall   on - ly   seem   to   re -

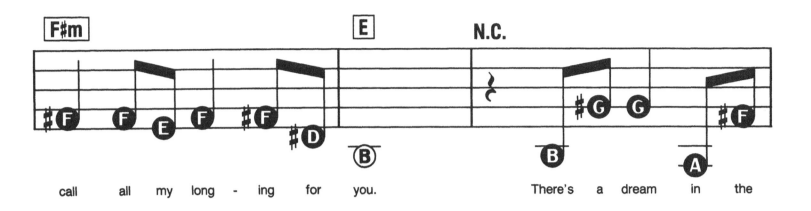

call all my long - ing for you. There's a dream in the

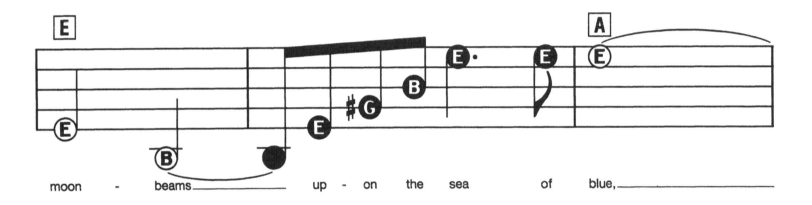

moon - beams_____ up - on the sea of blue,_____

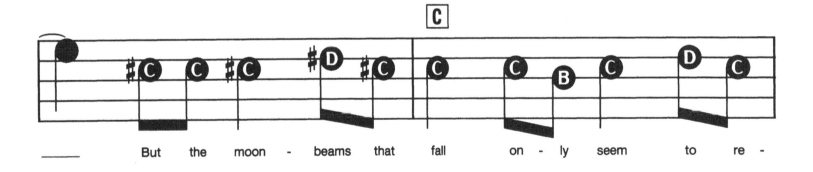

_____ But the moon - beams that fall on - ly seem to re -

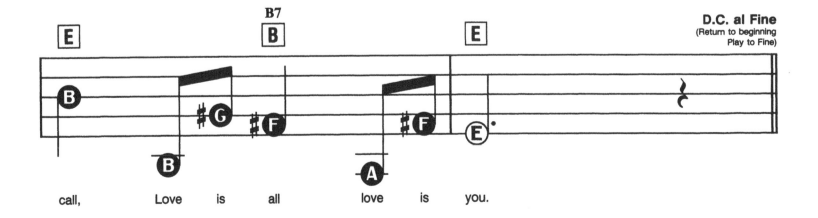

call, Love is all love is you.

D.C. al Fine
(Return to beginning
Play to Fine)

On The Street Where You Live

(From "MY FAIR LADY")

Registration 4
Rhythm: Beguine

Words by Alan Jay Lerner
Music by Frederick Loewe

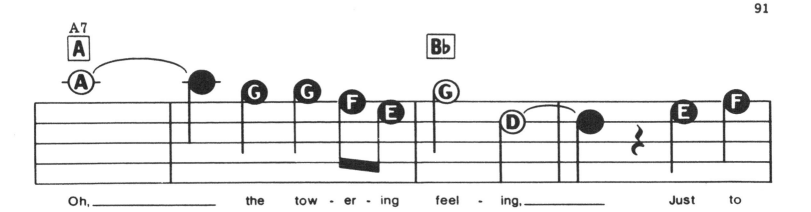

Oh, _____ the tow - er - ing feel - ing, _____ Just to

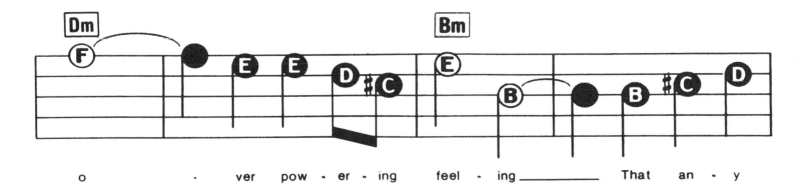

know _____ some - how you are near! _____ The

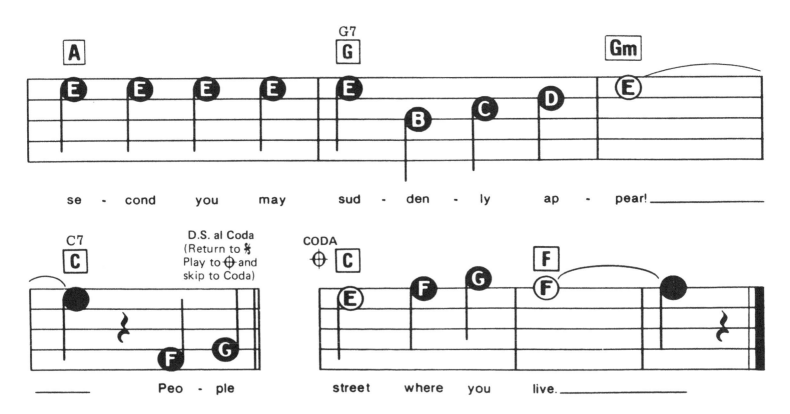

o - ver pow - er - ing feel - ing _____ That an - y

se - cond you may sud - den - ly ap - pear! _____

D.S. al Coda
(Return to 𝄋
Play to ⨁ and
skip to Coda)

_____ Peo - ple

street where you live. _____

The Poor People Of Paris
(Joan's Song)

Registration 4
Rhythm: Fox Trot

Original French words by Rene Rouzaud
English words by Jack Lawrence
Music by Marguerite Monnot

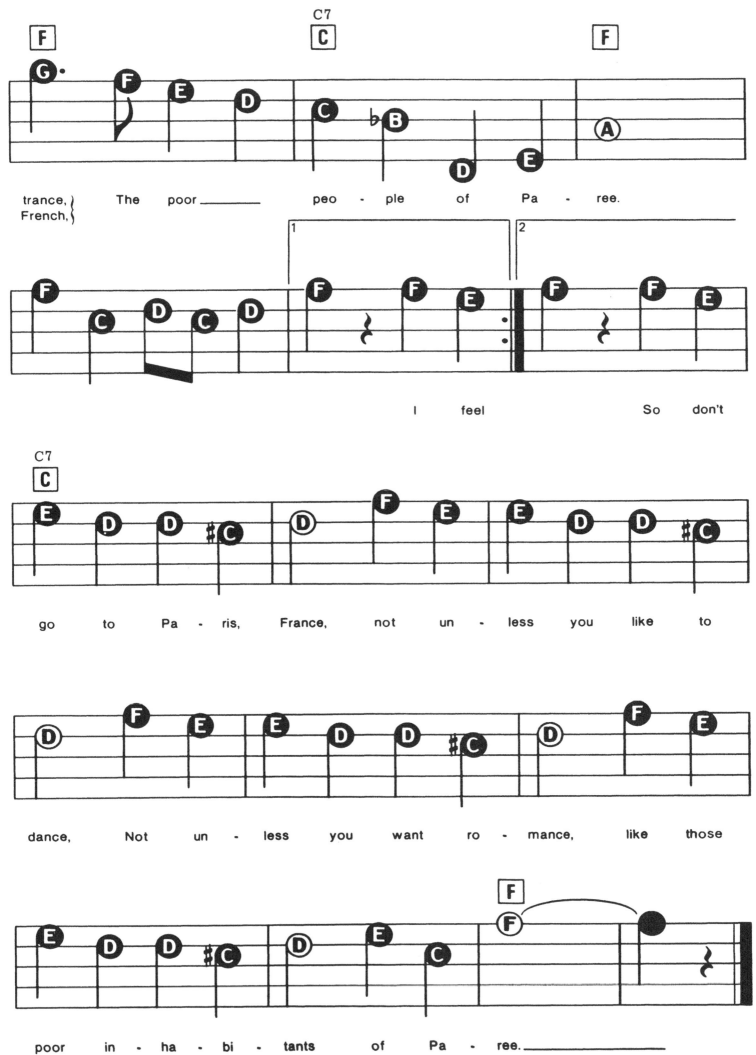

Primrose Lane

Registration 4
Rhythm: Swing or Jazz

Words and Music by
Wayne Shanklin and George Callender

Prim - rose Lane,   Life's a hol - i - day on

Prim - rose Lane,   Just a hol - i - day on

Prim - rose Lane   with____ you.____

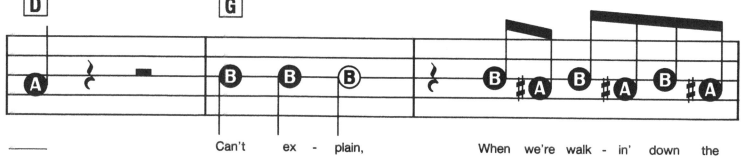

____ Can't ex - plain,   When we're walk - in' down the

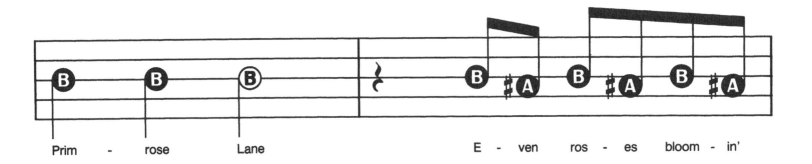

Prim - rose   Lane   E - ven ros - es bloom - in'

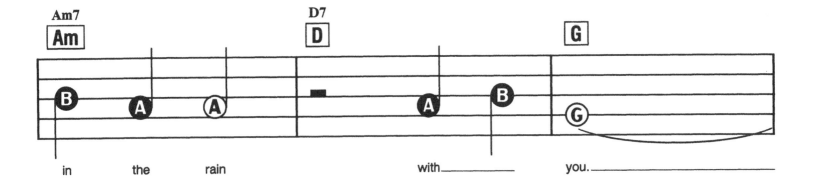

Am7 **Am**   **D7** **D**   **G**

in   the   rain   with_____   you._____

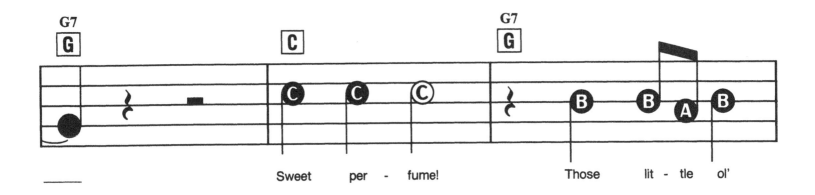

G7 **G**   **C**   **G7** **G**

_____   Sweet   per - fume!   Those   lit - tle   ol'

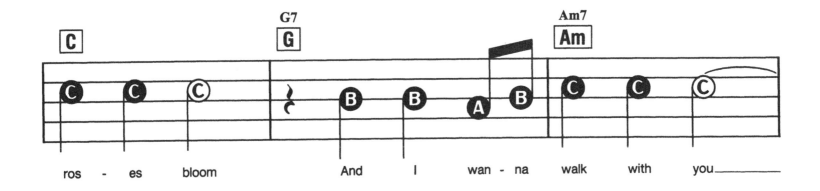

C   **G7** **G**   **Am7** **Am**

ros - es   bloom   And   I   wan - na   walk   with   you_____

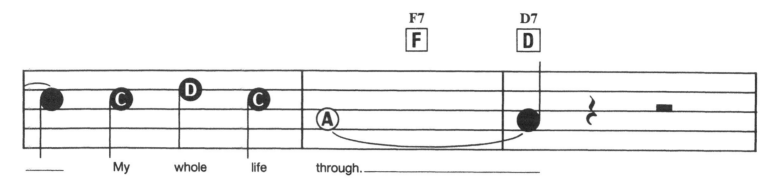

My whole life through.

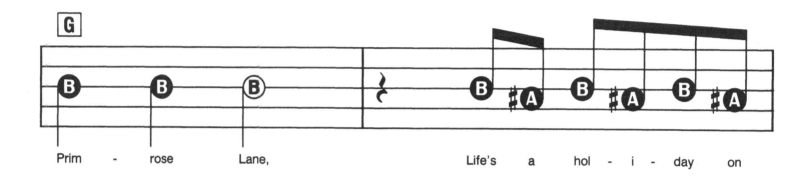

Prim - rose Lane, Life's a hol - i - day on

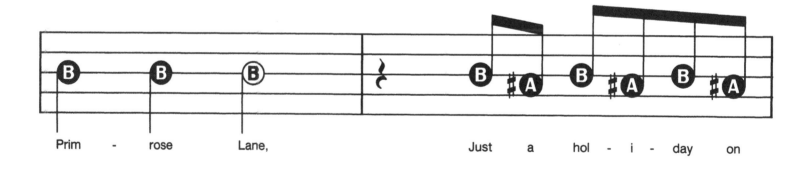

Prim - rose Lane, Just a hol - i - day on

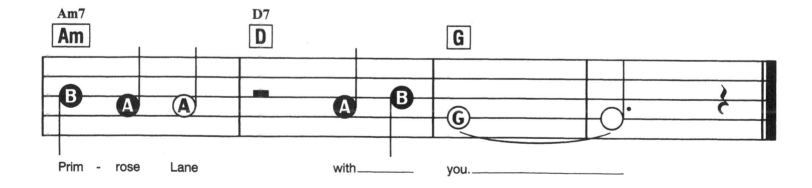

Prim - rose Lane with you.

She Didn't Say "Yes"

Registration 5
Rhythm: Fox Trot or Swing

Words and Music by
Jerome Kern

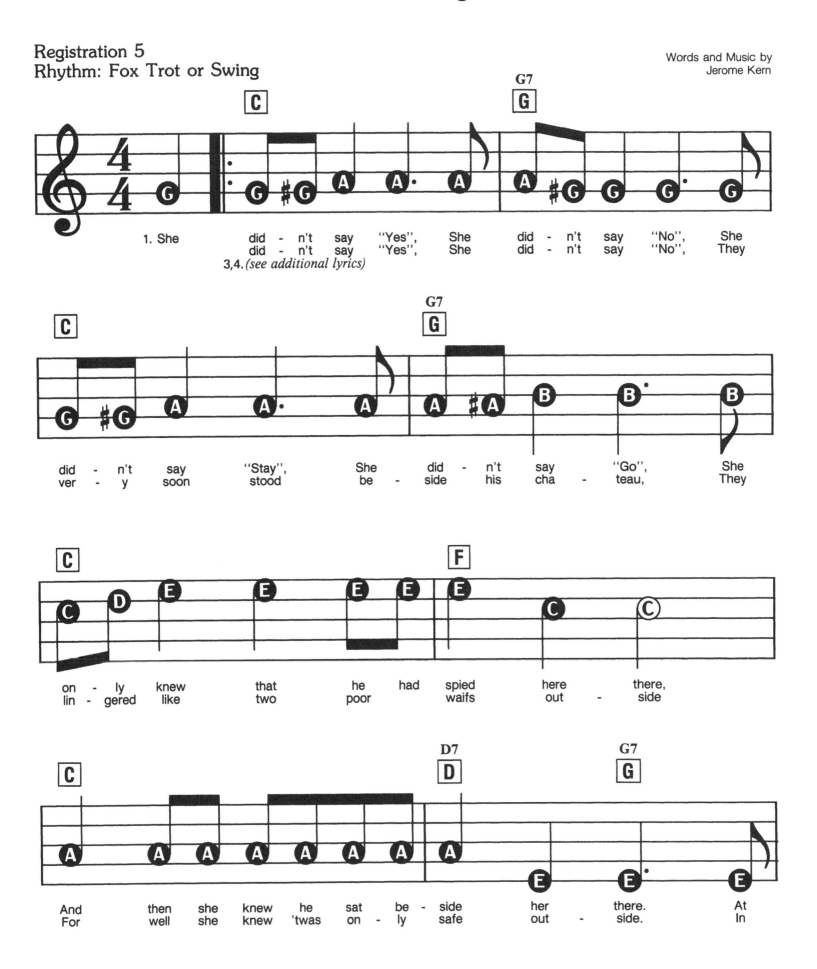

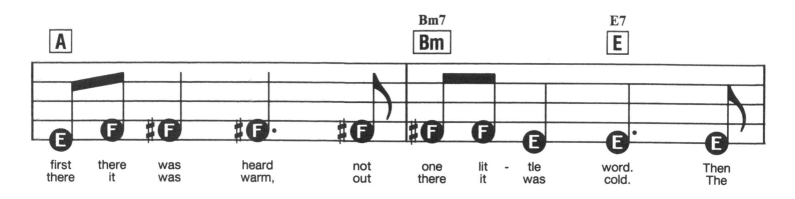

first there was heard not one lit - tle word. Then
there it was warm, out there it was cold. The

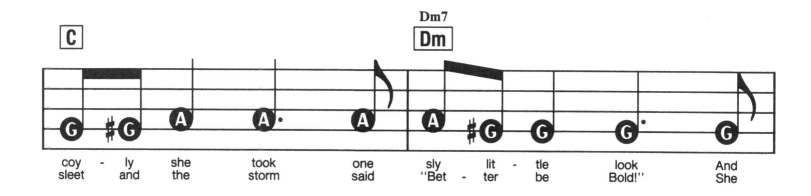

coy - ly she took one sly lit - tle look And
sleet and the storm said "Bet - ter be Bold!" She

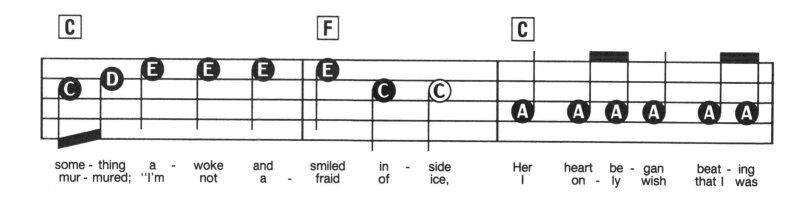

some - thing a - woke and smiled in - side, Her heart be - gan beat - ing
mur - mured; "I'm not a - fraid of ice, I on - ly wish that I was

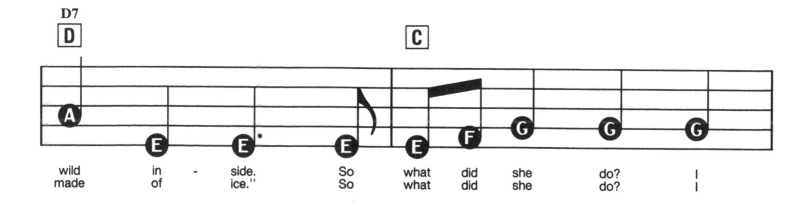

wild in - side. So what did she do? I
made of ice." So what did she do? I

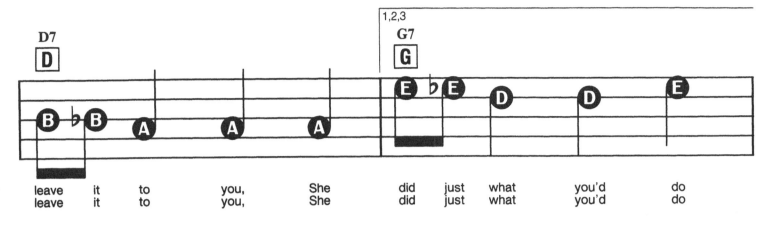

leave it to you, She did just what you'd do
leave it to you, She did just what you'd do

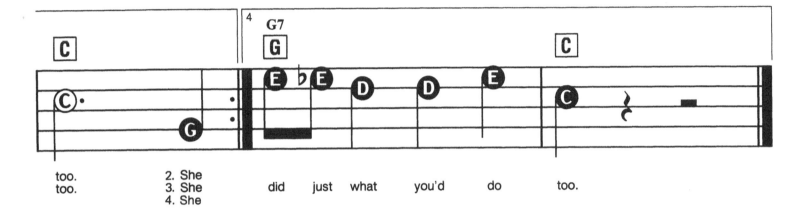

too. 2. She
too. 3. She did just what you'd do too.
4. She

Additional Lyrics

3. She didn't say "Yes," She didn't say "No,"
   She wanted to stay But knew she should go,
   She wasn't so sure that he'd be good,
   She wasn't even sure that she'd be good.
   She wanted to rest all cuddled and pressed
   A palpable part of somebody's heart.
   She loved to be "enrapport" with him,
   But not behind a bolted door with him.
   And what did she do? I leave it to you,
   She did just what you'd do too.

4. She didn't say "Yes," She didn't say "No,"
   For heaven was near, she wanted it so,
   Above her sweet love was beckoning,
   And yet she knew there'd be a reckoning.
   She wanted to climb, but dreaded to fall
   So bided her time and clung to the wall,
   She wanted to act adlibitum,
   But feared to lose her equilibrium.
   So what did she do? I leave it to you,
   She did just what you'd do too.

Row, Row, Row

Registration 5
Rhythm: Fox Trot or Swing

Words by William Jerome
Music by Jimmie V. Monaco

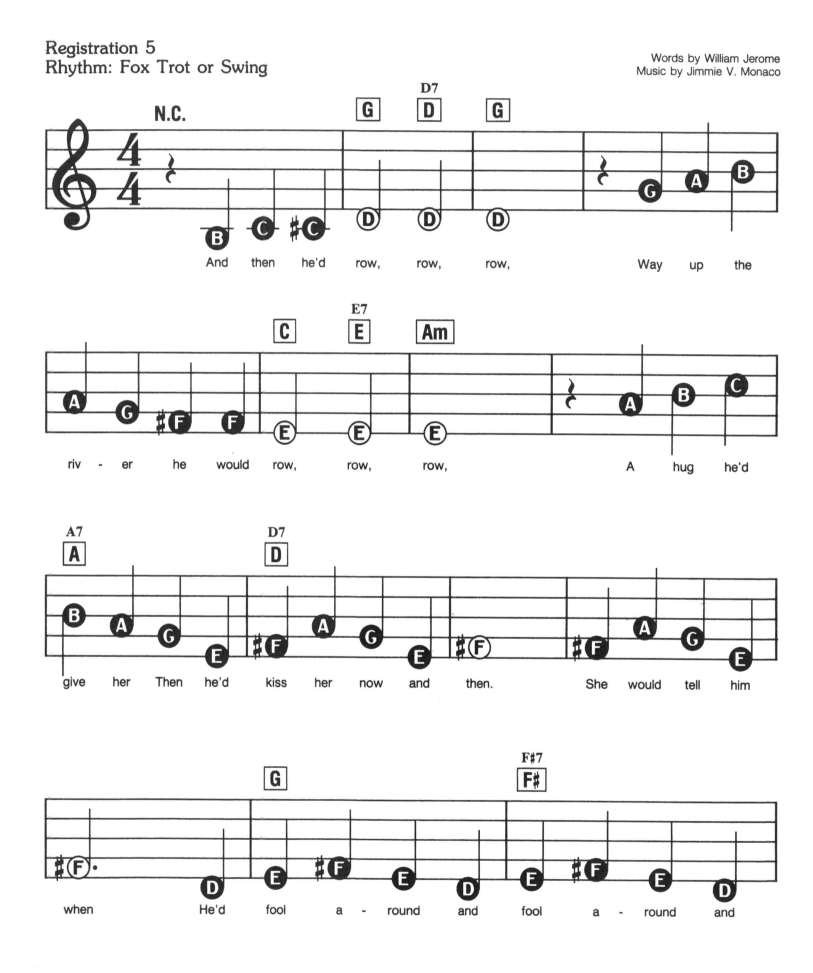

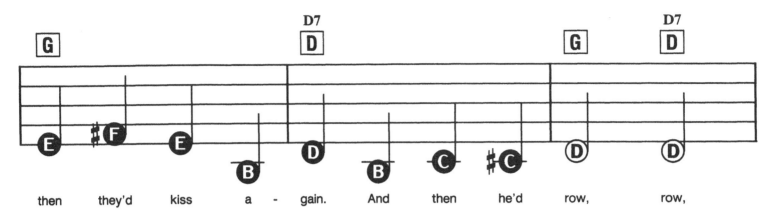

then they'd kiss a - gain. And then he'd row, row,

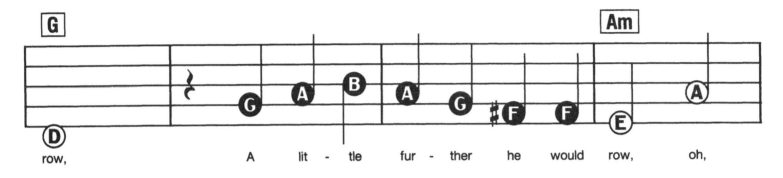

row, A lit - tle fur - ther he would row, oh,

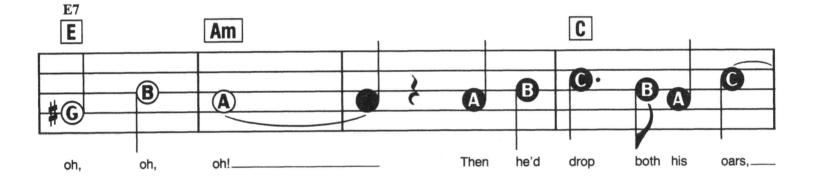

oh, oh, oh!_____ Then he'd drop both his oars,_____

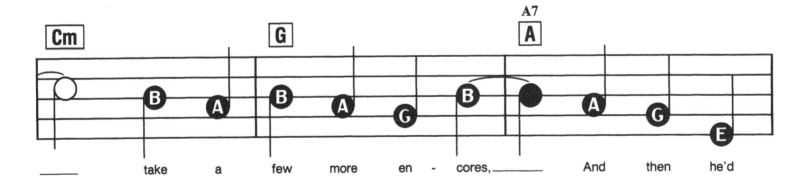

take a few more en - cores,_____ And then he'd

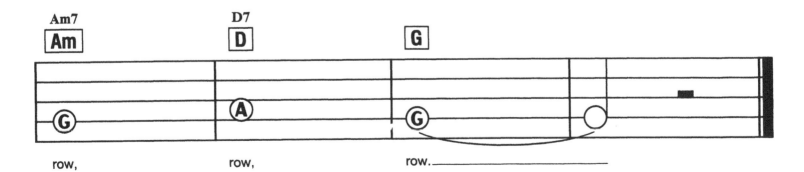

row, row, row._____

Smoke Gets In Your Eyes

Registration 10
Rhythm: Ballad or Swing

Words by Otto Harbach
Music by Jerome Kern

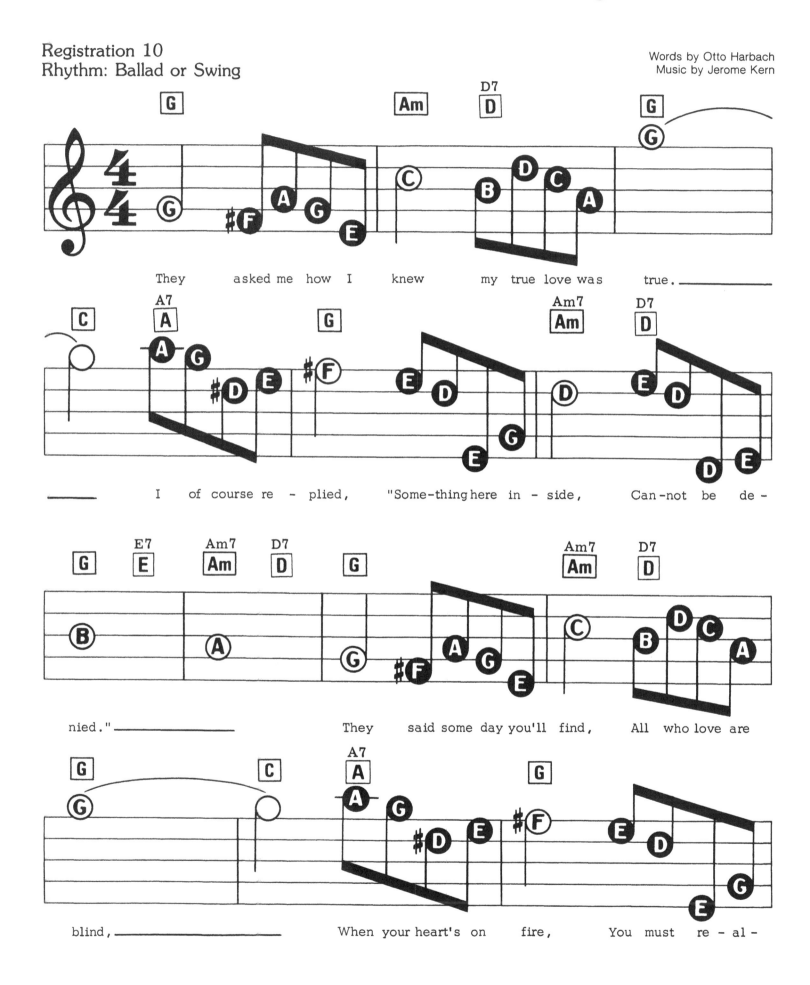

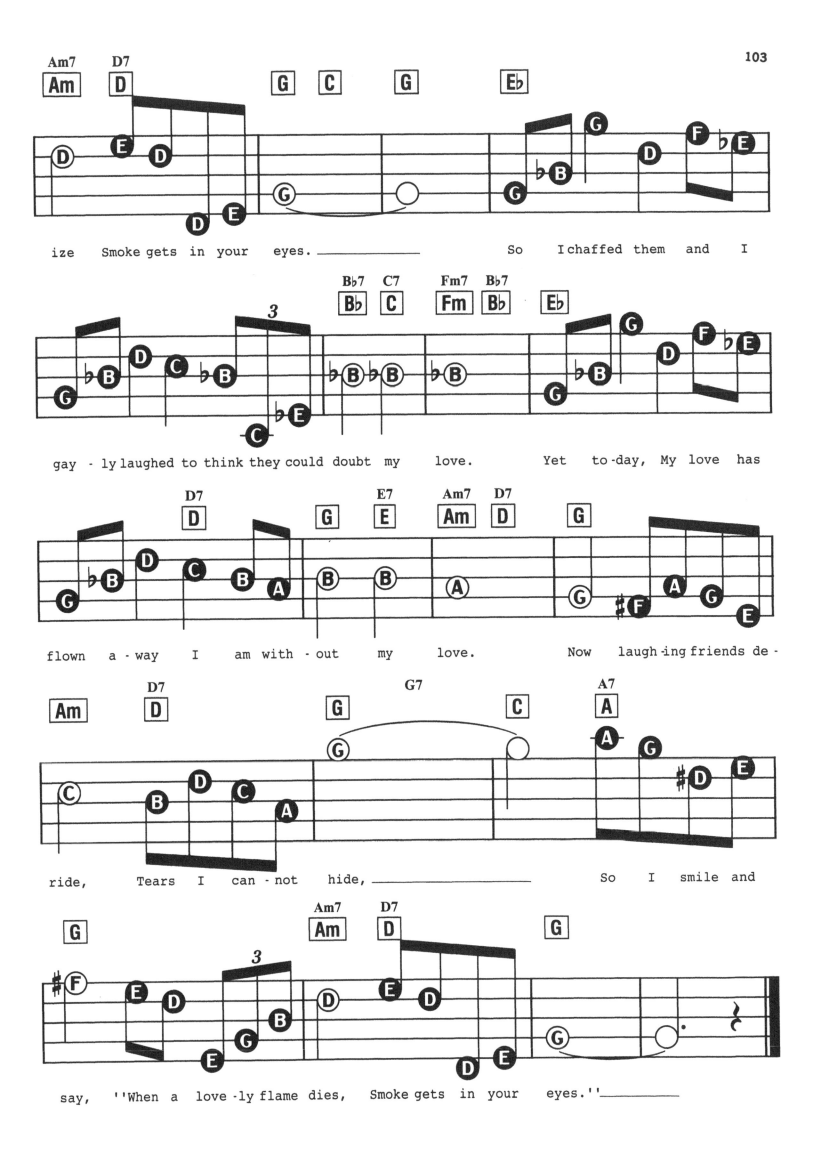

That's Life

Registration 7
Rhythm: Ballad or Swing

Words and Music by
Dean Kay and Kelly Gordon

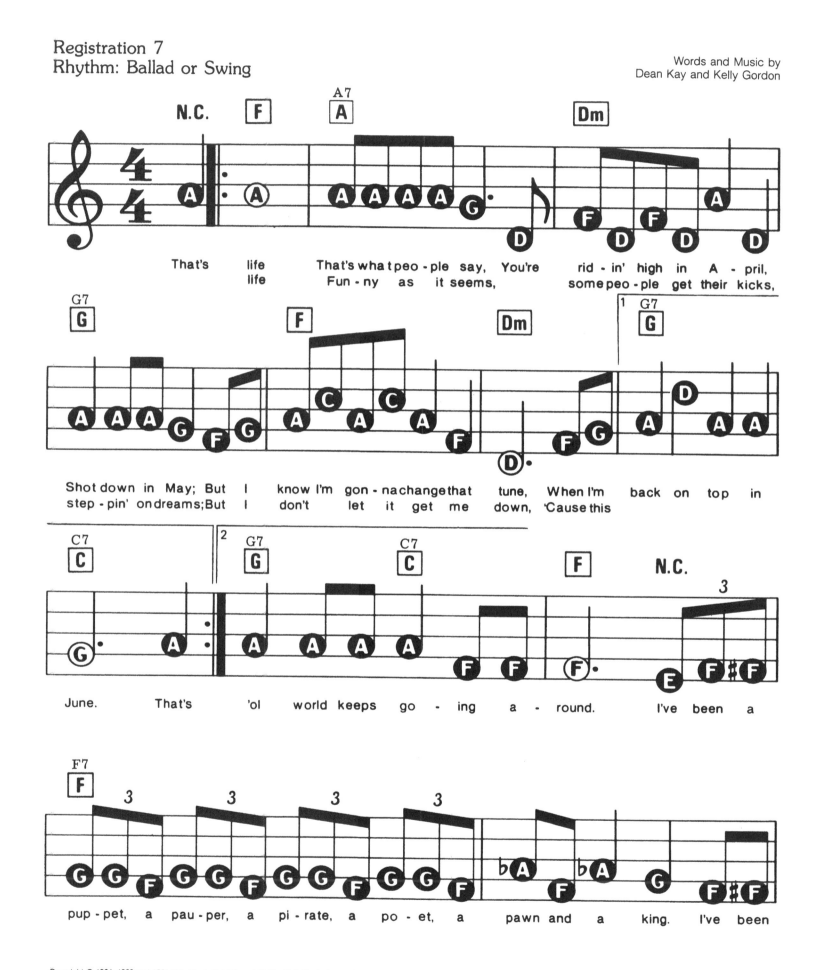

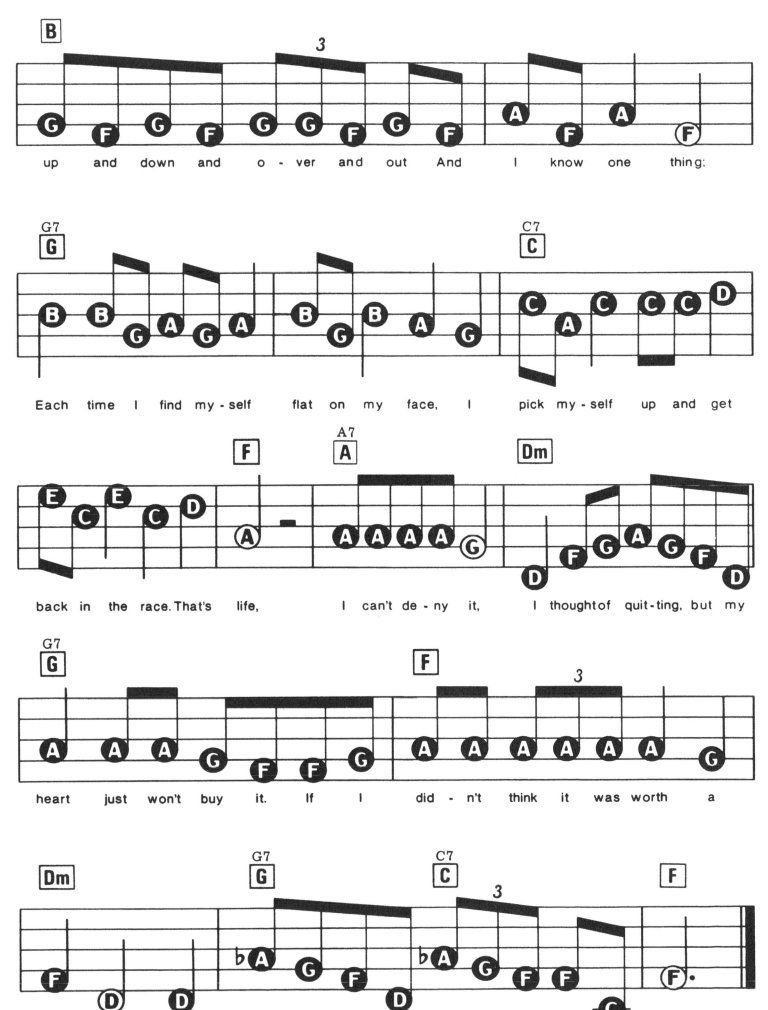

(There's Something About A) Hometown Band

Registration 4
Rhythm: 6/8 March

By John Nagy, Milt Lance
and Don Canton

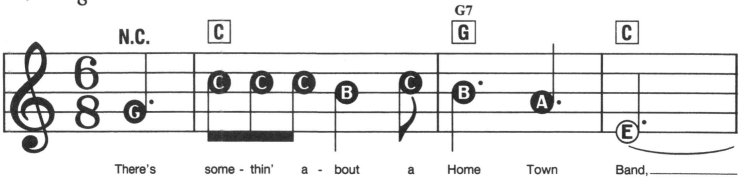

There's some-thin' a-bout a Home Town Band,

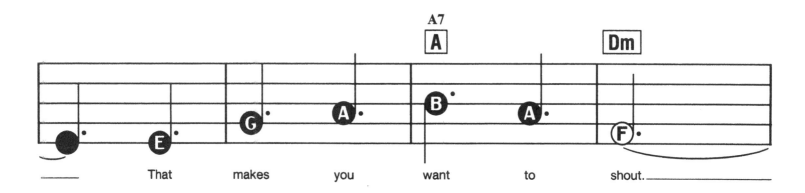

That makes you want to shout.

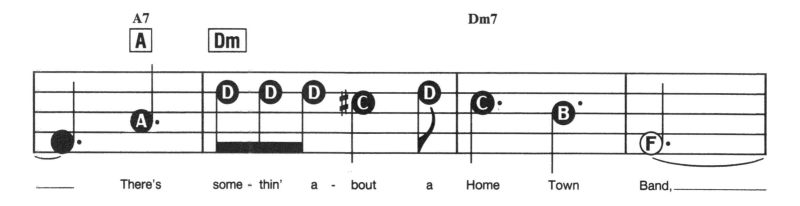

There's some-thin' a-bout a Home Town Band,

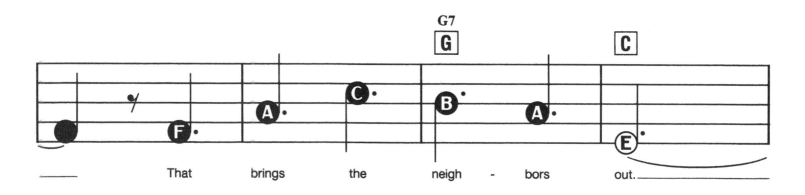

That brings the neigh-bors out.

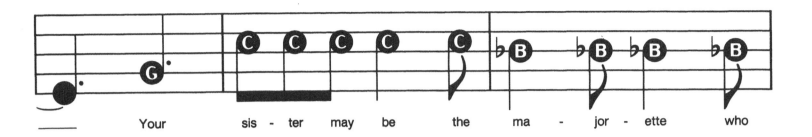

Your sis - ter may be the ma - jor - ette who

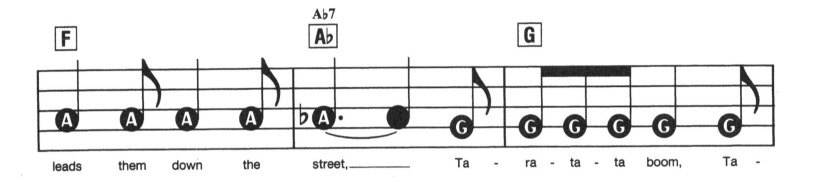

leads them down the street,_____ Ta - ra - ta - ta boom, Ta -

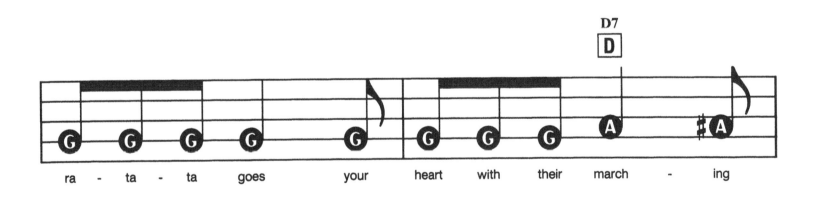

ra - ta - ta goes your heart with their march - ing

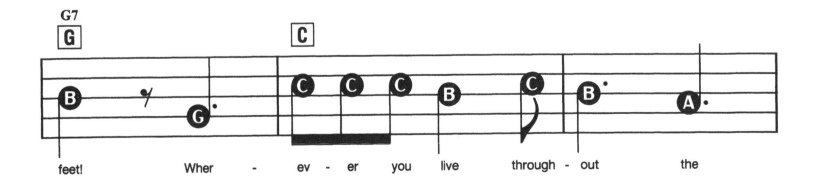

feet! Wher - ev - er you live through - out the

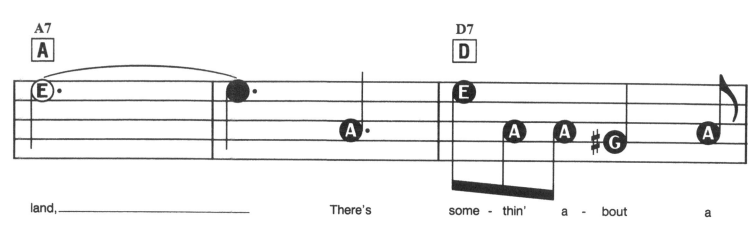

land,_____ There's some - thin' a - bout a

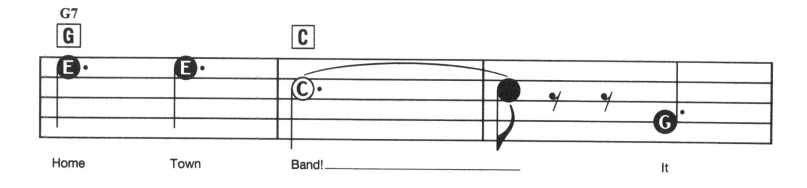

Home Town Band!_____ It

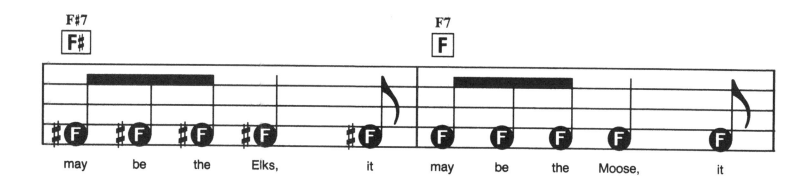

may be the Elks, it may be the Moose, it

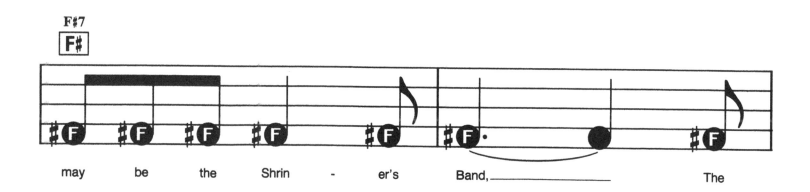

may be the Shrin - er's Band,_____ The

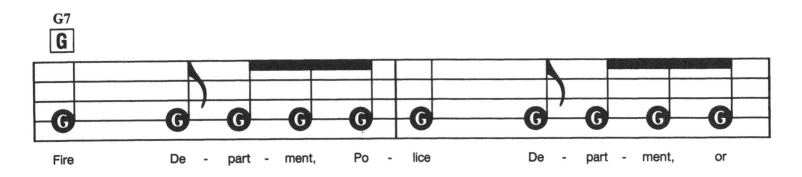

Fire De - part - ment, Po - lice De - part - ment, or

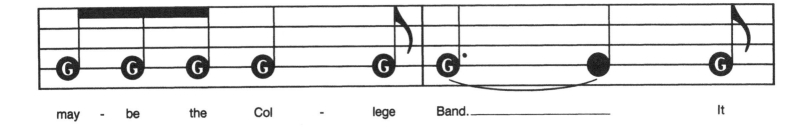

may - be the Col - lege Band._____ It

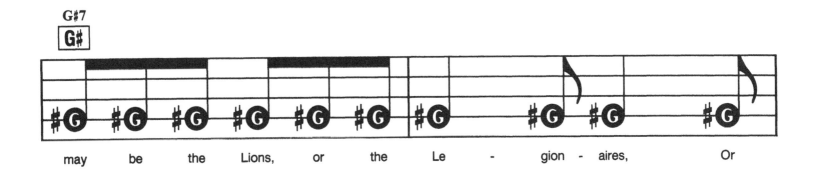

may be the Lions, or the Le - gion - aires, Or

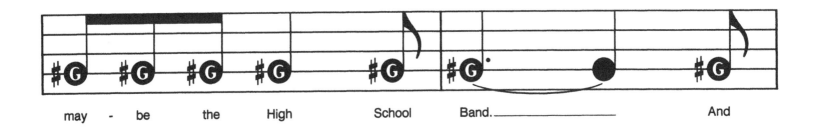

may - be the High School Band._____ And

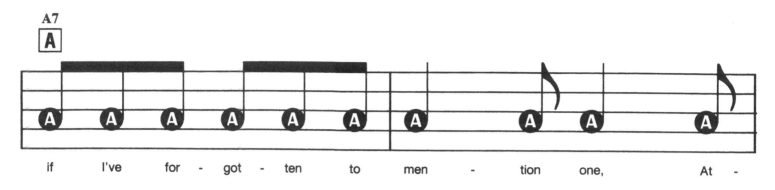

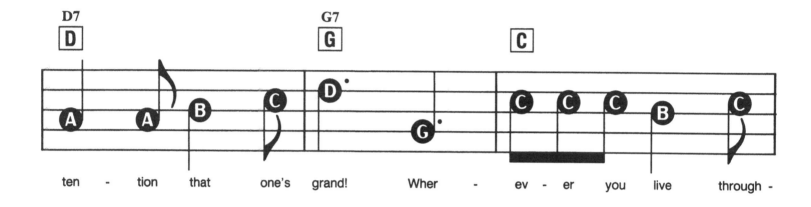

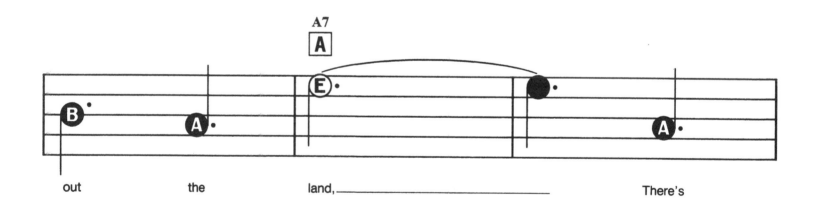

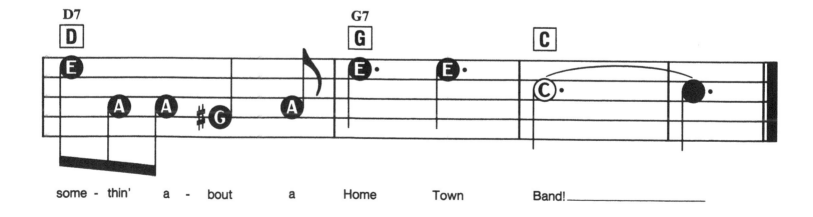

The Touch Of Your Hand

Registration 4
Rhythm: Waltz

Words by Otto Harbach
Music by Jerome Kern

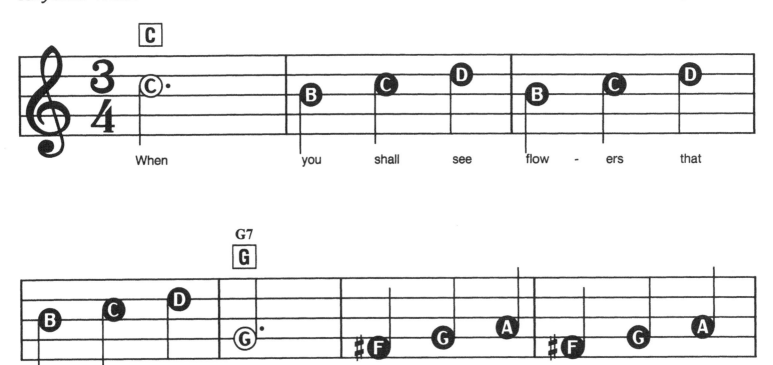

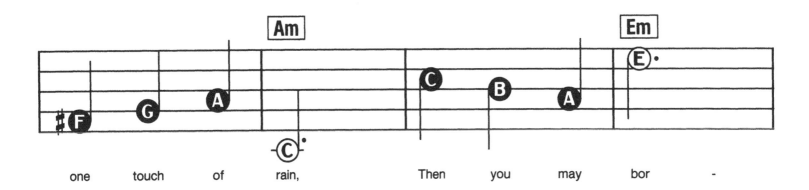

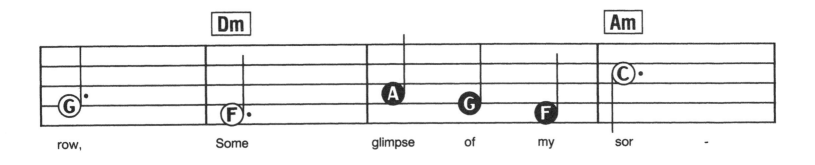

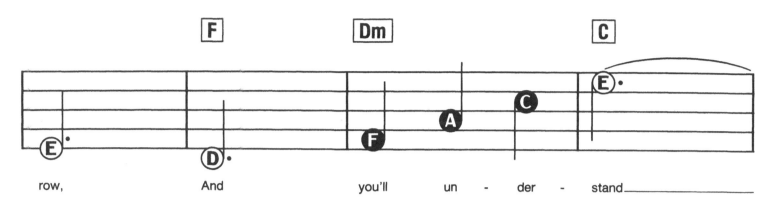

row,　　　　　　And　　　　　you'll　un - der - stand_____

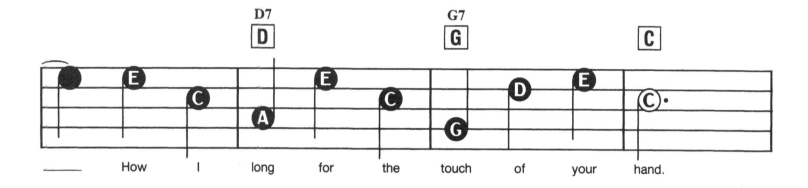

_____　　How　I　long　for　the　touch　of　your　hand.

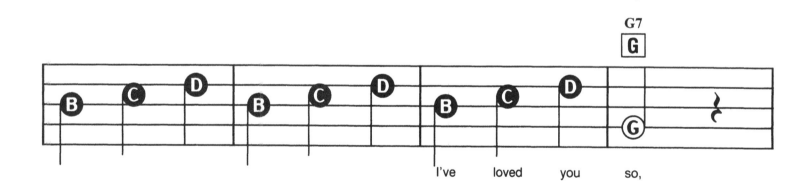

I've　loved　you　so,

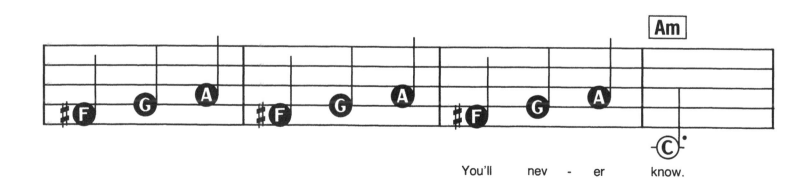

You'll　nev - er　know.

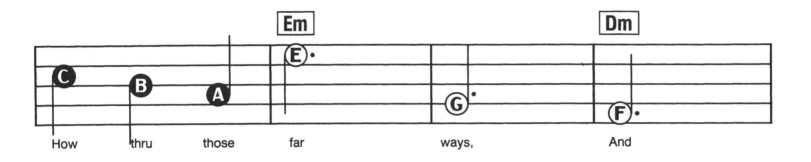

How thru those far ways, And

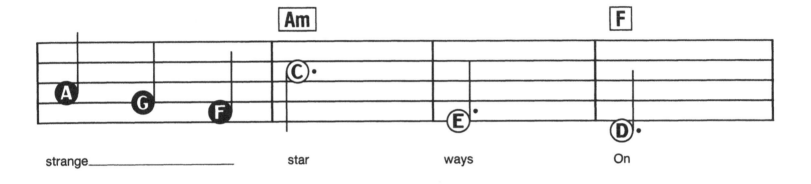

strange_____ star ways On

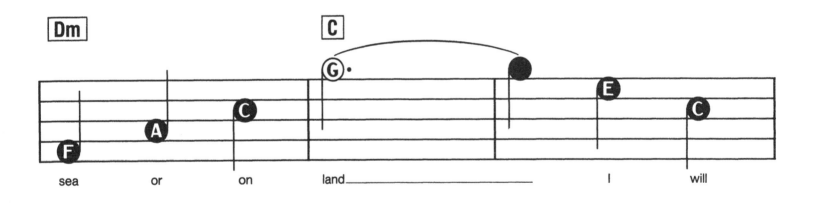

sea or on land_____ I will

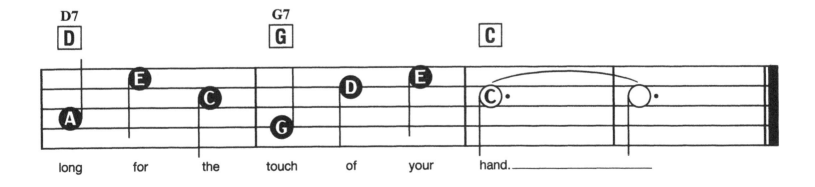

long for the touch of your hand._____

They Didn't Believe Me

Registration 2
Rhythm: Ballad or Swing

Words by Herbert Reynolds
Music by Jerome Kern

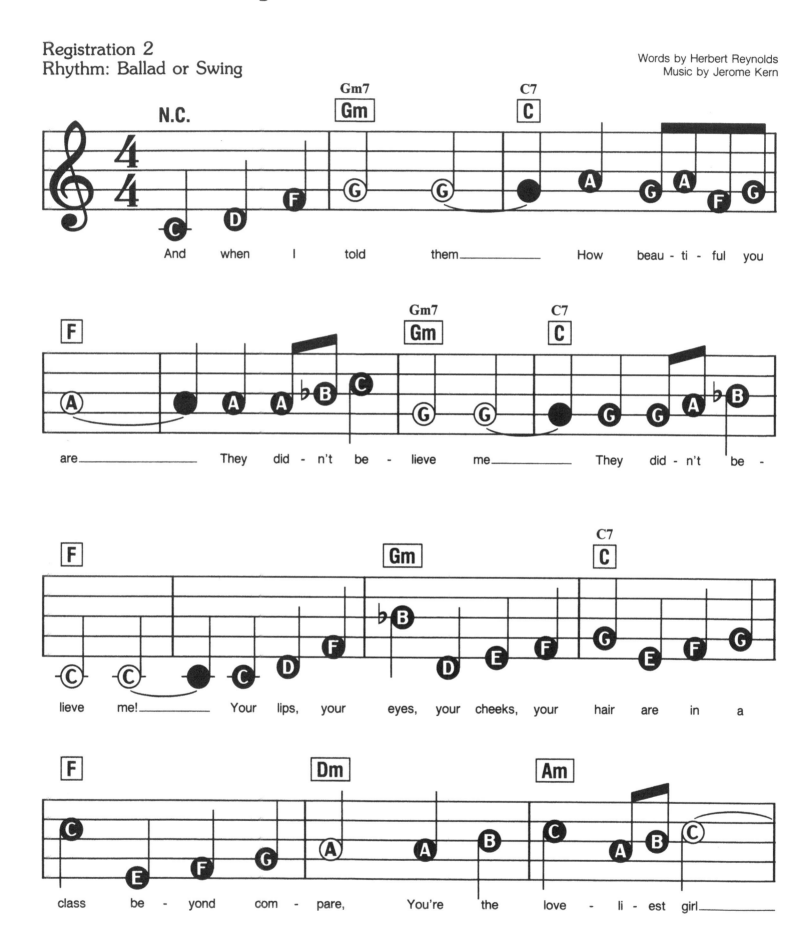

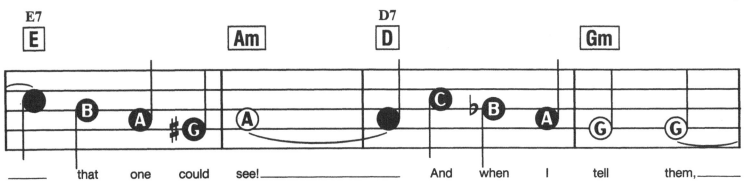

that one could see! And when I tell them,

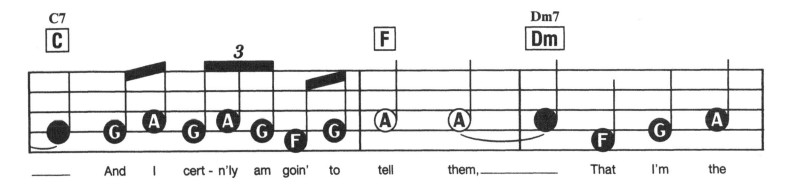

And I cert-n'ly am goin' to tell them, That I'm the

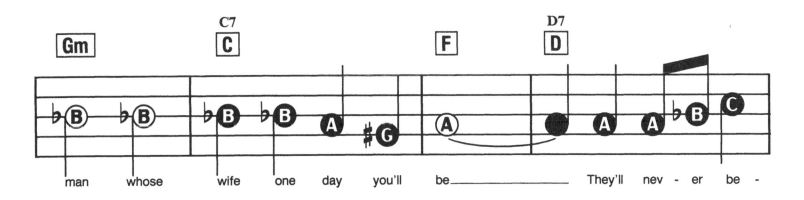

man whose wife one day you'll be They'll nev-er be-

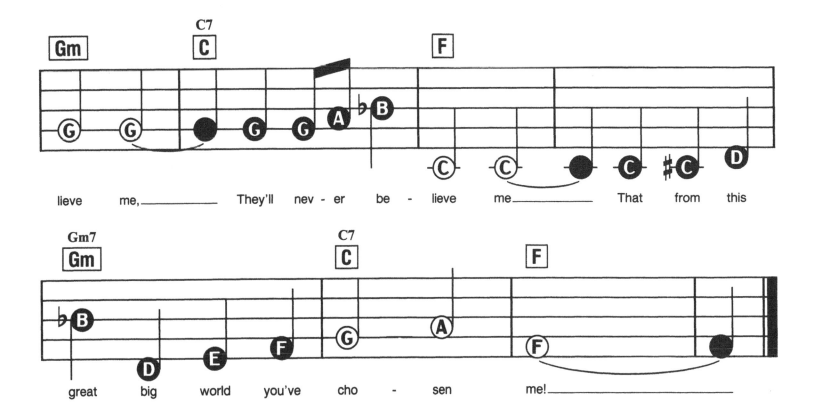

lieve me, They'll nev-er be-lieve me That from this

great big world you've cho-sen me!

Watch What Happens

English Words by Norman Gimbel
Music by Michel Legrand

Registration 2
Rhythm: Bossa Nova or Latin

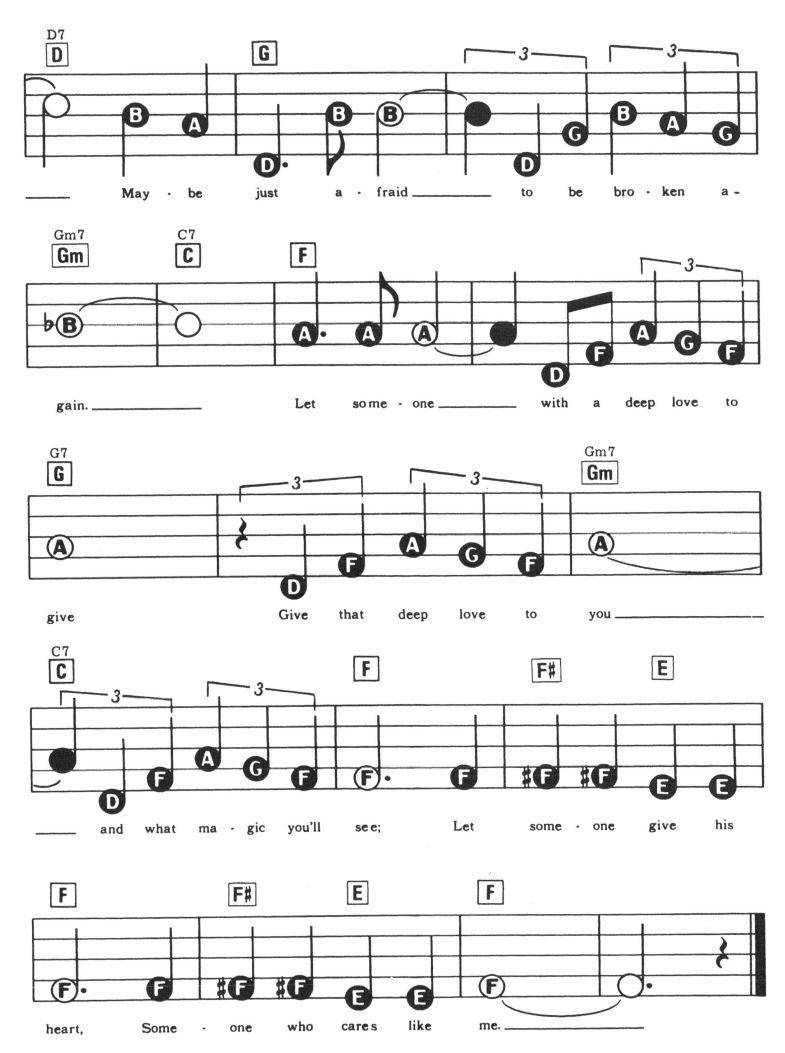

The Way You Look Tonight

Registration 3
Rhythm: Fox Trot or Swing

Words by Dorothy Fields
Music by Jerome Kern

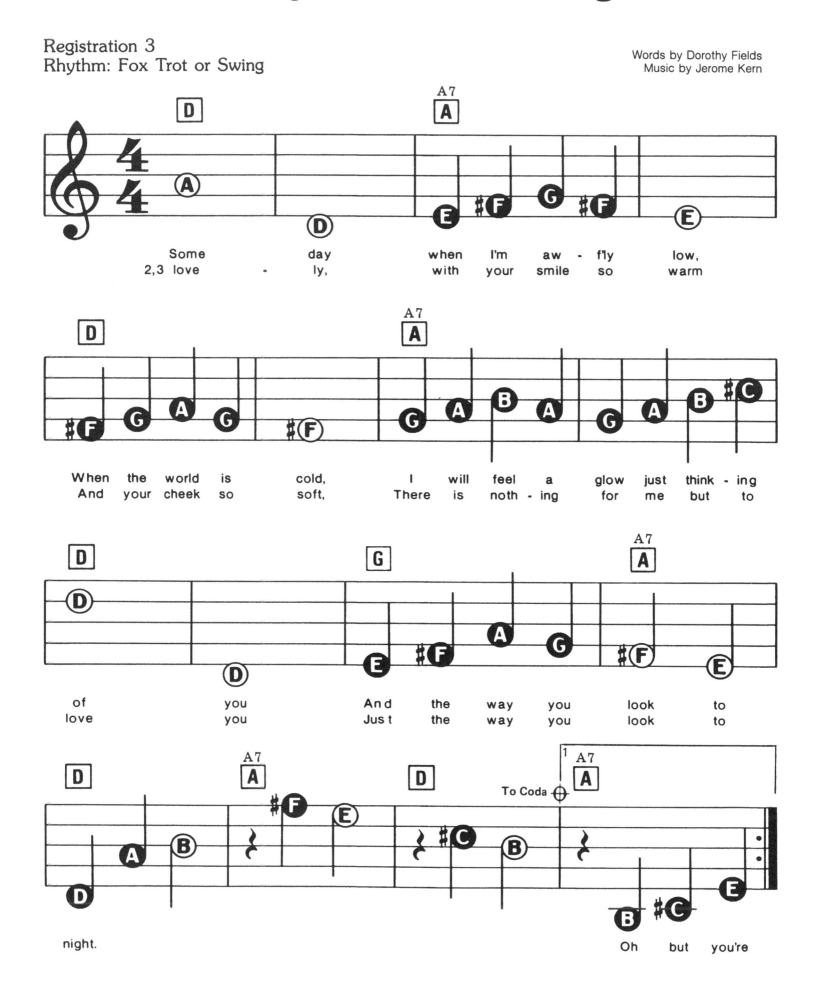

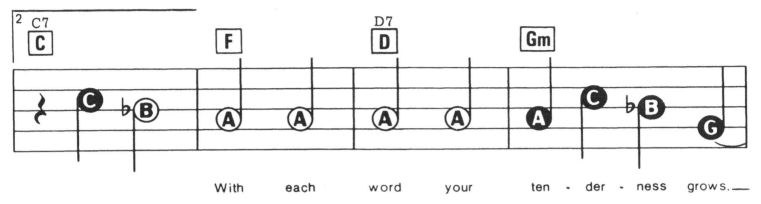

With each word your ten - der - ness grows._____

_____ tear - ing my fear_____ a - part,_____

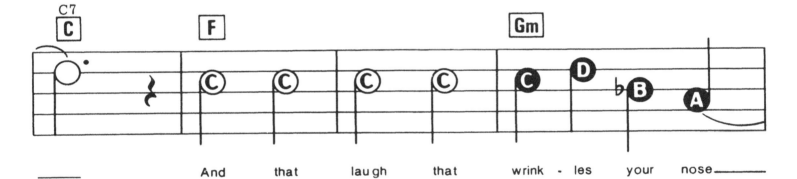

_____ And that laugh that wrink - les your nose_____

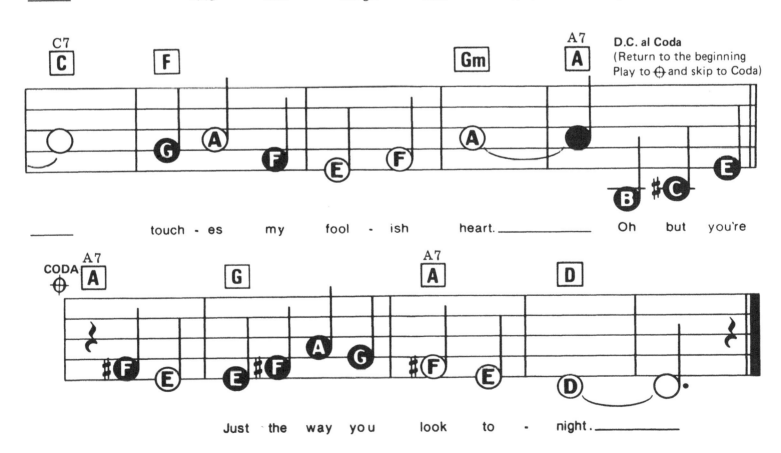

_____ touch - es my fool - ish heart._____ Oh but you're

Just the way you look to - night._____

The Wayward Wind

Registration 4
Rhythm: Country or Shuffle

Words and Music by
Herb Newman and Stan Lebowsky

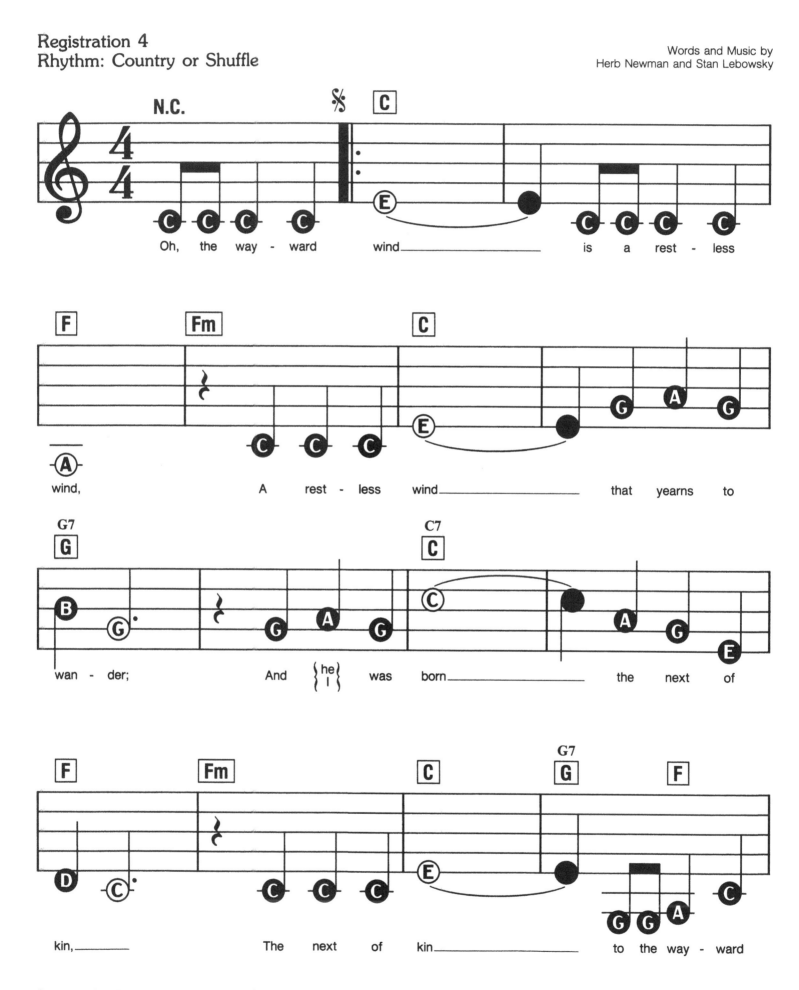

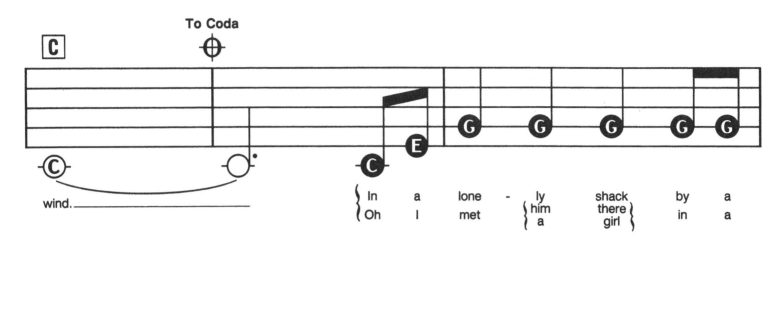

To Coda

wind._____

In a lone - ly shack by a
Oh I met him a shack there a girl in a

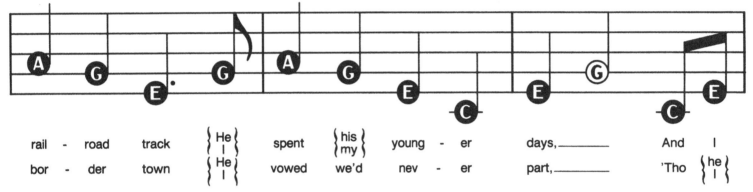

rail - road track He spent his young - er days,_____ And I
bor - der town He I vowed we'd nev - er part,_____ 'Tho he

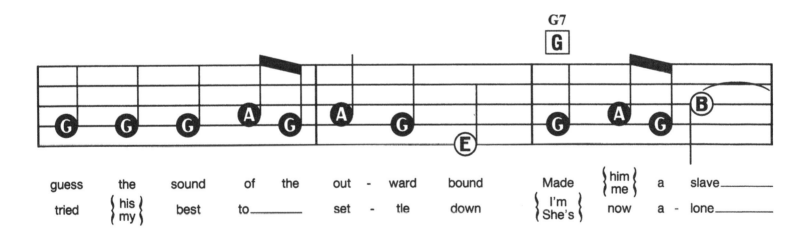

G7

guess the sound of the out - ward bound Made him a slave_____
tried his best to_____ set - tle down I'm now a - lone_____
my She's

2nd time D.S. al Coda
(Return to %
Play to ⊕ and
skip to Coda)

CODA

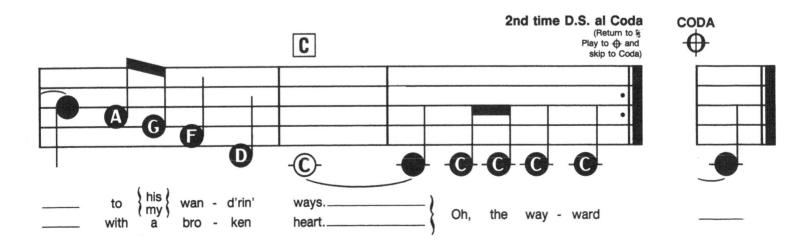

____ to his wan - d'rin' ways._____
my
____ with a bro - ken heart._____ Oh, the way - ward

When My Baby Smiles At Me

Registration 1
Rhythm: Fox Trot or Swing

By Harry Von Tilzer, Andrew B. Sterling,
Bill Munro and Ted Lewis

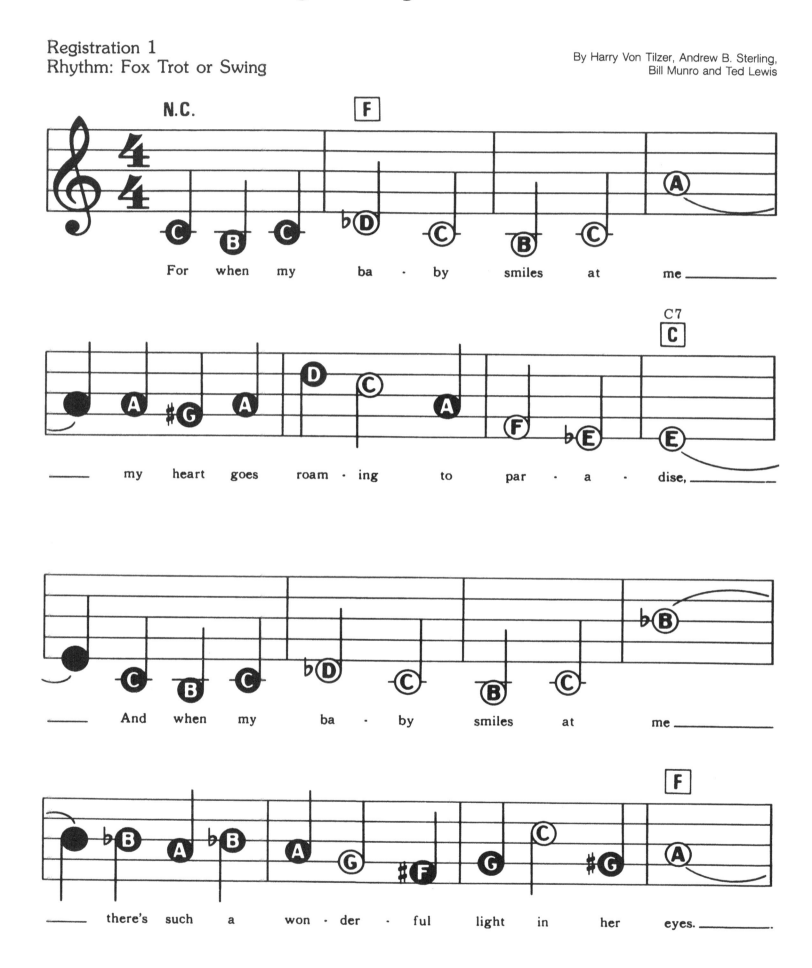

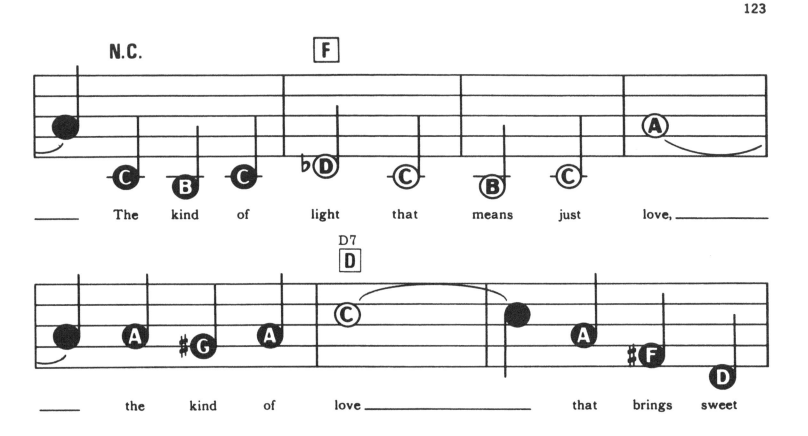

The kind of light that means just love, _____ the kind of love _____ that brings sweet

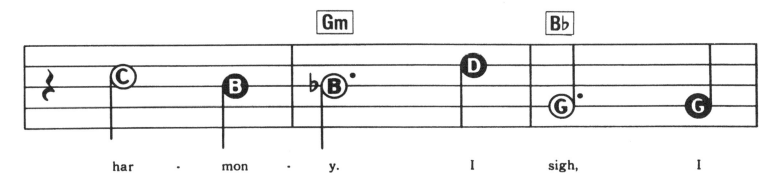

har · mon · y. I sigh, I

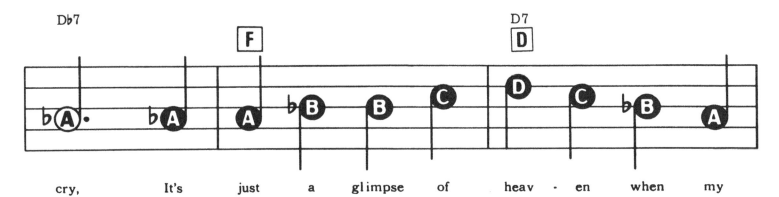

cry, It's just a glimpse of heav · en when my

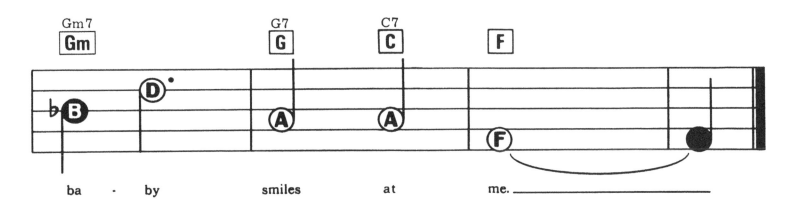

ba · by smiles at me. _____

Who?

Registration 1
Rhythm: Fox Trot or Swing

Words by Otto Harbach and Oscar Hammerstein II
Music by Jerome Kern

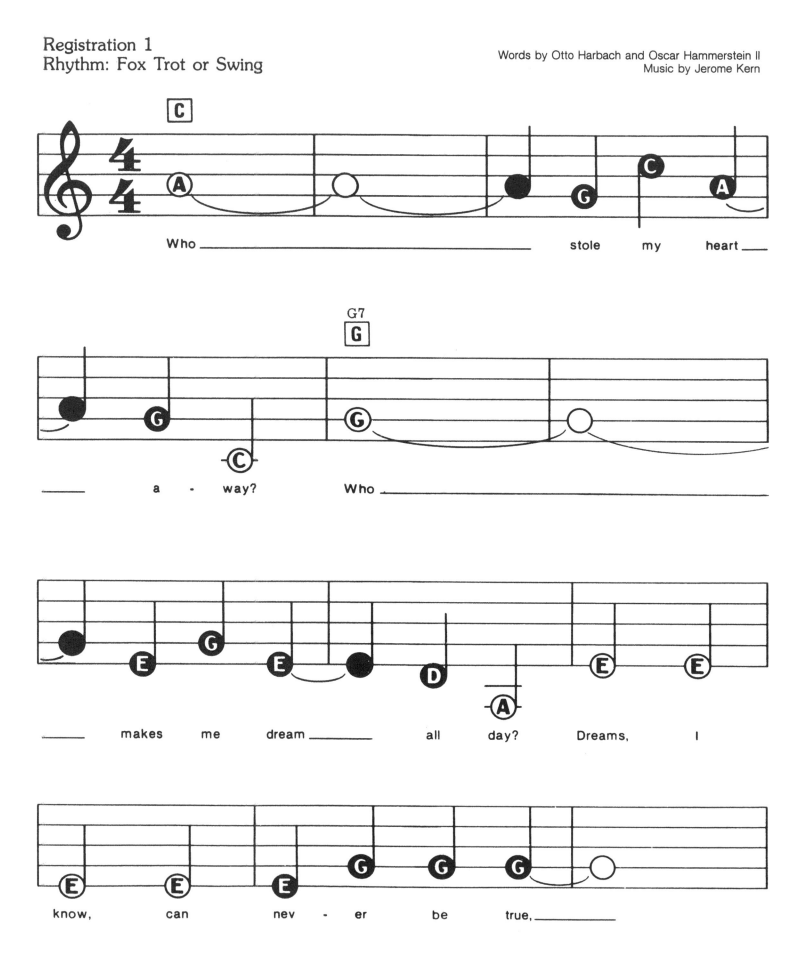

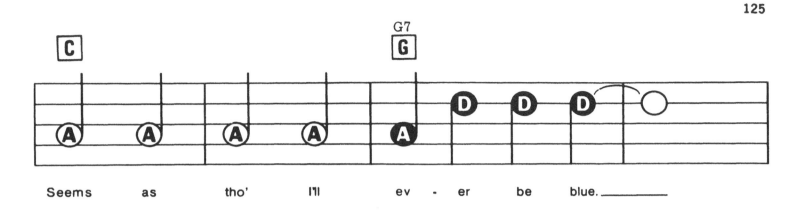

Seems as tho' I'll ev - er be blue. _____

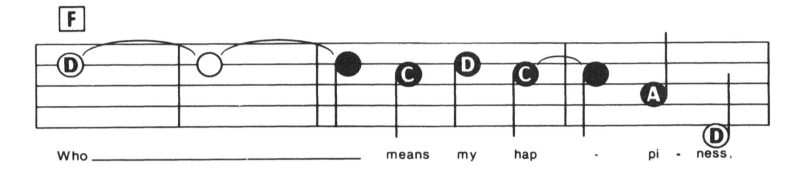

Who _____ means my hap - pi - ness,

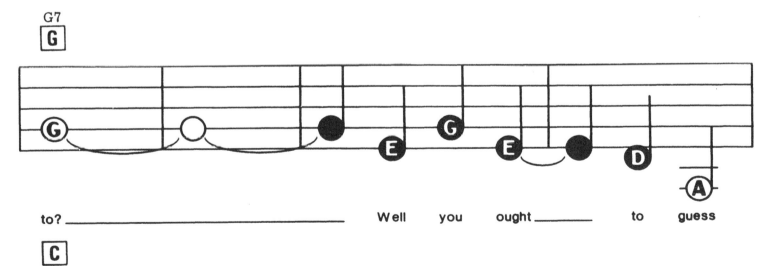

Who _____ would I an - swer: yes,

to? _____ Well you ought ____ to guess

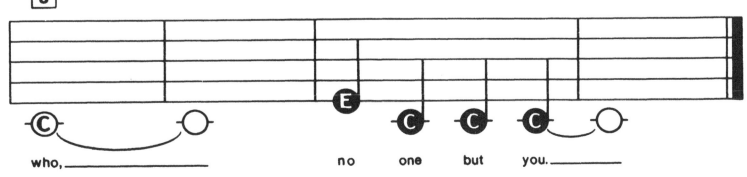

who, _____ no one but you. _____

Yellow Bird

Words by Marilyn Keith and Alan Bergman
Music by Norman Luboff

Registration 4
Rhythm: Rhumba or Latin

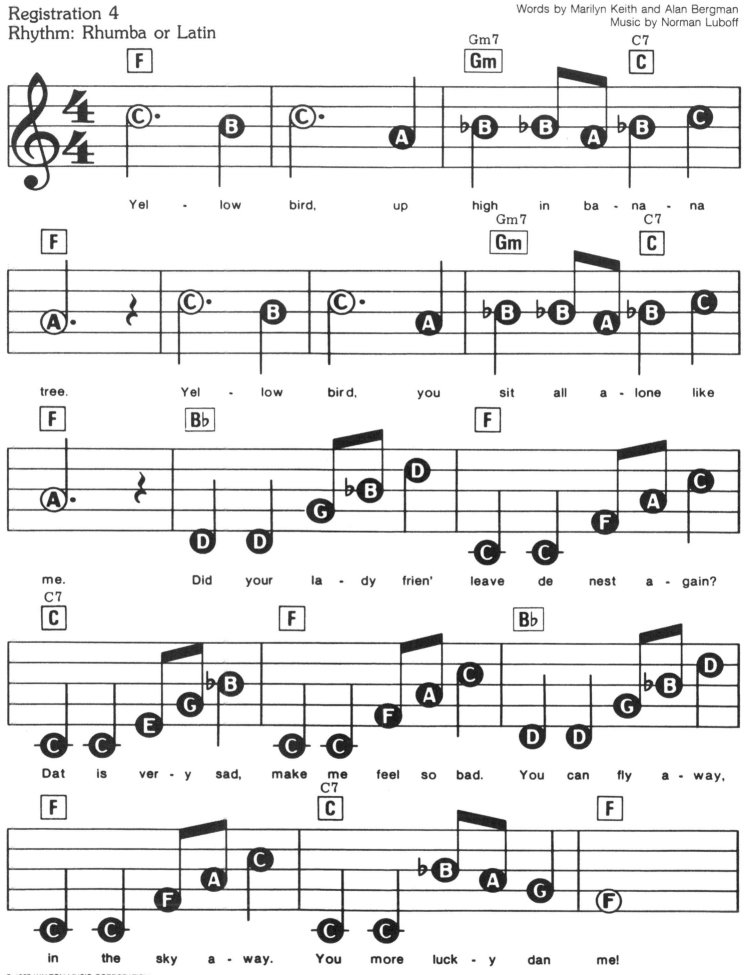

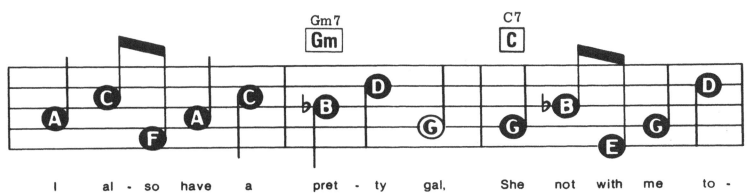

I al - so have a pret - ty gal, She not with me to -

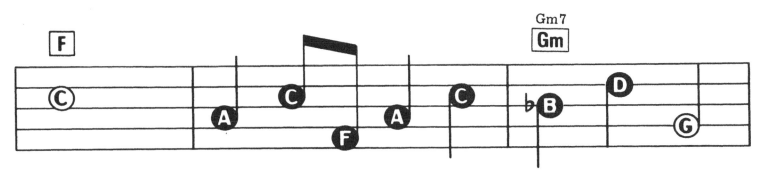

day. Dey all de same, de pret - ty gal,

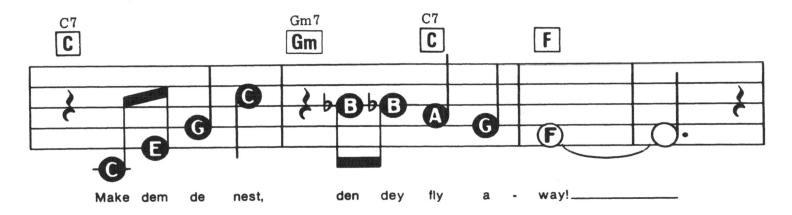

Make dem de nest, den dey fly a - way!_____

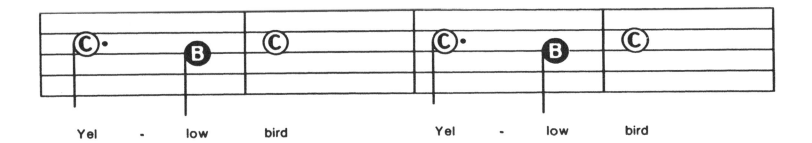

Yel - low bird Yel - low bird

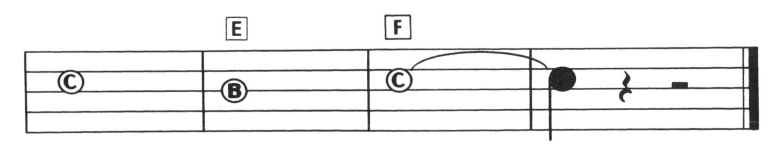

Yel - low bird._____

E-Z Play® TODAY Registration Guide
For All Organs

On the following chart are 10 numbered registrations for both tonebar (TB) and electronic tab organs. The numbers correspond to the registration numbers on the E-Z Play TODAY songs. Set up as many voices and controls listed for each specific number as you have available on your instrument. For more detailed registrations, ask your dealer for the E-Z Play TODAY Registration Guide for your particular organ model.

REG. NO.		UPPER (SOLO)	LOWER (ACCOMPANIMENT)	PEDAL	GENERALS
1	Tab	Flute 16', 2'	Diapason 8' Flute 4'	Flute 16', 8'	Tremolo/Leslie – Fast
	TB	80 0808 000	(00) 7600 000	46, Sustain	Tremolo/Leslie – Fast (Upper/Lower)
2	Tab	Flute 16', 8', 4', 2', 1'	Diapason 8' Flute 8', 4'	Flute 16' String 8'	Tremolo/Leslie – Fast
	TB	80 7806 004	(00) 7503 000	46, Sustain	Tremolo/Leslie – Fast (Upper/Lower)
3	Tab	Flute 8', 4', 2⅔', 2' String 8', 4'	Diapason 8' Flute 4' String 8'	Flute 16', 8'	Tremolo/Leslie – Fast
	TB	40 4555 554	(00) 7503 333	46, Sustain	Tremolo/Leslie – Fast (Upper/Lower)
4	Tab	Flute 16', 8', 4' Reed 16', 8'	Flute 8', (4) Reed 8'	Flute 8' String 8'	Tremolo/Leslie – Fast
	TB	80 7766 008	(00) 7540 000	54, Sustain	Tremolo/Leslie – Fast (Upper/Lower)
5	Tab	Flute 16', 4', 2' Reed 16', 8' String 8', 4'	Diapason 8' Reed 8' String 4'	Flute 16', 8' String 8'	Tremolo/Leslie
	TB	40 4555 554 Add all 4', 2' voices	(00) 7503 333	57, Sustain	
6	Tab	Flute 16', 8', 4' Diapason 8' String 8'	Diapason 8' Flute 8' String 4'	Diapason 8' Flute 8'	Tremolo/Leslie – Slow (Chorale)
	TB	45 6777 643	(00) 6604 020	64, Sustain	Tremolo/Leslie – Slow (Chorale)
7	Tab	Flute 16', 8', 5⅓', 2⅔', 1'	Flute 8', 4' Reed 8'	Flute 8' String 8'	Chorus (optional) Perc Attack
	TB	88 0088 000	(00) 4333 000	45, Sustain	Tremolo/Leslie – Slow (Chorale)
8	Tab	Piano Preset or Flute 8' or Diapason 8'	Diapason 8'	Flute 8'	
	TB	00 8421 000	(00) 4302 010	43, Sustain	Perc Piano
9	Tab	Clarinet Preset or Flute 8' Reed 16', 8'	Flute 8' Reed 8'	Flute 16', 8'	Vibrato
	TB	00 8080 840	(00) 5442 000	43, Sustain	Vibrato
10	Tab	String (Violin) Preset or Flute 16' String 8', 4'	Flute 8' Reed 8'	Flute 16', 8'	Vibrato or Delayed Vibrato
	TB	00 7888 888	(00) 7765 443	57, Sustain	Vibrato or Delayed Vibrato

NOTE: TIBIAS may be used in place of FLUTES. VIBRATO may be used in place of LESLIE.